INSIDE THE GATES OF HEAVEN

ODEN HETRICK

INSIDE THE GATES
OF HEAVEN

THIS BOOK IS DEDICATED
TO A MAN SENT FROM GOD WHOSE NAME IS JOHN
AND TO MY DEDICATED FAMILY

Revelation 22:14

**Blessed are they that do
his commandments, that
they may have right to the
tree of Life, and may enter
in through the gates, into
the City.**

INSIDE THE GATES OF HEAVEN
CONTENTS

PART TWO: Testimony of the Family

PART THREE

3

FOREWORD

Those whom God Sovereignly chooses to visit the portals of Heaven have always fascinated me. The vast majority of these men or women will never grace the cover of a national magazine, nor be invited to sit with the "who's who" on Christian TV. For the simple reason God still chooses the weak things of the world to shame the wise and mighty, while the world continues to look for a superstar. The one straightforward reason for this is: No flesh shall glory in His Presence. Humility required.

I believe Oden Hetrick fulfilled these qualifications. Though he was a man who visited Heaven over eighty times he still carried the humbleness of greatness. In an interview I heard him say while he had forgotten many things here on earth, he never forgot anything he was shown in Heaven. These are the things our Heavenly Father desires to reveal to us all, the place He prepared for you and me!

Of the many books I have read on Heaven I can honestly say this is my favorite. I love the simplicity in which it is written, and the understanding of revelation I came away with. It was as though I traveled with him on his journey from the outer courts to the very majestic and holy Throne Room of the Father God. Like me, you will begin to experience the sights and sounds of our eternal home creating the insatiable longing for His Presence now, not just later.

For those who are purely looking for a theological treatise you may well be disappointed. This isn't merely about information of a far off paradise for the Christian in the sweet by and by. This is about a holy longing for more of Jesus. It is about more of the King and His Kingdom. It is about the unimaginable love that not only saved us *from hell,* but also saved us *to Heaven*. With each page you will be drawn into the magnificence of such holy love and the unexplainable greatness of our God!

This isn't a one time read book. I've read it multiple times and with each reading I see something I haven't seen before. For all of those who hunger for the realms of Glory now, allow Oden Hetrick's visitations to begin to satisfy your craving. I promise you will come away only desiring more of Him. This is a journey you will want to relive over and over again. This is "prepare to meet Thy God!"

Eddie T Rogers
Author and founder
Revival In Power
Revival Alliance International Network - RAIN

OTHERS WHO WERE BLESSED

Inside the Gates of Heaven is one of the most compelling accounts of an individuals encounters with God in this generation. Not only does this account take you on a journey through the gates of glory, it answers some of the questions long asked by many about our eternal destination. I have personally read and re-read this account in light of what the Lord is revealing to many of us in this hour and find that Brother Oden was a forerunner for many of us. His words and experiences have been repeated through many others who have had similar experiences. The Lord is truly trying to encourage this generation with the reality that awaits all of us - Heaven, our eternal destiny.

Bruce Allen

For those unsure of the existence of Heaven, Oden Hetrick's detailed account of his visits to the place we all long for serves as a true doubt-demolisher and faith-injector. The fact that Oden led an exemplary righteous, Christian life lends further credence to his written testimony. It was my honor both to have known him as a friend and to have been inspired by his great faith.

Steve Jones

Extra Mile Ministries

www.extramileministries.net

The Hetrick family is very special to me. They adopted me into their family like a daughter and sister, and have blessed me in many ways. Dad Hetrick was a genuine man of God with a gentle spirit. I trust you will be blessed and edified by what the Lord has revealed to him. I look forward to experiencing the exciting glories of Heaven soon that he has left on record for our encouragement and instruction.

Arlene A. Cober

My very *spirit* and *soul* were moved to the core by Mr. Hetrick's sacred visits to the Kingdom of God. After reading this book your walk with Yahshua will never be the same. What a beautiful gift Mr. Hetrick has given us... a sacred loving glimpse into what awaits us in heaven!

Joy Schulz

When I read the reports of dreams and vision given by Holy Spirit to people today, I know that I am not reading *Scripture* like I read in the Bible. But, whenever I read these reports Holy Spirit always speaks to me. And, Holy Spirit spoke to me when I read this book.

Pastor Carl Hahn

"Inside the Gates of Heaven is an insightful and educational look into the Heavenly realm. Reading of Brother Oden's experiences gives me the desire to be taken there to see and experience it for myself."

Pastor Dean Wood

Comfort and Light Ministries

HOW THIS BOOK CAME TO BE
By David Hetrick

From earliest childhood, my Dad, Oden Hetrick knew that he was being watched over by an invisible guardian angel. He knew that he was delivered many times throughout his lifetime by supernatural intervention from accidents, evil men and death.

At the age of twelve he accepted Jesus as his Savior from sin. Thereafter, he looked forward to living in Heaven forever.

Due to this background and years of Bible study with fasting and prayer, he was not afraid when three angels appeared to him in the power of the Spirit of God and took him on his first visit to Heaven. Then, over a period of about 40 years, God granted him the privilege of visiting Heaven often, not out of his body, but in the Spirit just as men of the Bible visited Heaven and the Throne of God.

Dad compared with Scripture the things he saw and learned. He also read accounts of others who visited the City of God, and found a remarkable agreement in all the ways God has made known His eternal Habitation.

Through the years Dad told our family about the beauties and delights of Heaven and the glories of God's Throne. In the spring of 1985, God instructed that this Heaven message be made known to this generation. It's like our mother once said, "You've got to be heavenly-minded if you're going to be any earthly good." Therefore we are pleased to offer this book to the reading public.

What we have seen and heard declare we unto you. 1 John 1:3

We look not at things that are seen, but at the things that are not seen: for the things that are seen are temporal; but the things that are not seen are eternal. II Cor 4:18

INTRODUCTION

WHAT IS THE TRUTH? Every person in this world sooner or later arrives at a theory of life that he will live, and die by. But everyone does not find the truth.

There are many simple truths of life that we accept without question, but it is of utmost importance that we discover and possess the Eternal Truth. This is not found in things, but in a person, the Son of God -- who came to restore us to favor with God.

"Jesus said, I Am the way, the <u>truth</u>, and the life; no man cometh unto the Father but by me. John 14:6

Again Jesus said.   "....I tell you the <u>truth</u>..." John 8:45

We read from books that Columbus discovered America for us. This is the knowledge of things unseen. It's easy to believe (accept) because we do not have to act upon this truth. But when we learn that Jesus is God's Son, and that He died on the cross for us, we have difficulty, because believing this requires that we change our theory of life and humbly repent of our sins.

Jesus said, "....if you believe not that I Am, you shall *die in your sins." John 8:24

(*to die in your sins is to be separated forever from God who is life.)

When the Bible tells us that Jesus is the Divine Son of God, it is giving us the knowledge of things unseen. This is faith, for faith is knowing what we cannot see. *[Faith is the confident assurance of what*

11

we hope for, the proof of unseen spiritual realities.] As you read the Bible, and this book, you will be increasing your faith, for you will learn about things we hope for but do not see. Whether you accept and believe these things or not is up to you, but some day you will have to give an account to God of what you did with this knowledge.

For we must all appear before the judgment seat of Christ; that every one may receive the things done in his body, according to that he hath done, whether it be good or bad. II Corinthians 5:10

...it is appointed unto men once to die, but after this the judgment. Hebrews 9:27

Many things prove to us that Jesus spoke the truth. All time is dated from His birth. We also have preserved for us in the Bible seven eye-witness accounts of what Jesus said and did. *(I don't think the department stores sell eye--witness accounts of Columbus discovering America!)* Jesus said He would heal the sick -- and He did. He said He would raise the dead -- and He did. He said He would rise from the dead on the third day -- and He did! He said He would return to this Earth as its Judge. Will your theory of life stand the test on that judgment day? Faith is knowing the truth. Accepting this truth is believing, and all things are possible to him that believeth. Jesus says to those who believe on Him,

"....you shall know the truth, (Jesus) and the truth (Jesus) shall make you free."

John 8:32

If the Son therefore shall make you free, you shall be free indeed." John 8:36

Oden Hetrick

PART ONE

Testimony of Oden Hetrick

Chapter I

ANGELS FROM HEAVEN

It would take a very long time for me to describe all of my visits to Heaven. So for this reason, we will take an imaginary journey to that Celestial City and I will be your guide. Along the way I will answer questions that have been frequently asked by those interested in their eternal Home.

My first understanding of God's unseen creation took place when I was in an army hospital with a sprained back. I had read my Bible and prayed, the lights were turned out, so I faced the wall and closed my eyes to sleep. Immediately, I saw ten angels around my bed. They were seven feet tall with large masculine bodies, beautiful faces, long golden hair and long white shining garments, that rustled like taffeta material. Their presence was so real, but when I opened my eyes to see them better, I saw no angels. Puzzled, I again faced the wall away from the angels, and as soon as my natural eyes were closed the angels were visible as before. Only with my physical eyes closed could I see the angels and feel their presence, because God had opened the eyes of my spirit to behold the invisible world where He lives.

A few years later, after graduating from Bible School and having fasted and prayed for what God would have me do, Jesus Himself appeared to my spirit in my study. I was told to learn how to love. Thinking that I knew how to love I was desirous to love someone with all my ability.

With these thoughts and desires I was then taken in spirit to paradise. There I met two masculine and three feminine beings. The six of us were under a tree talking, and decided to go to meet Jesus. We had not gone far until we found him and embraced Him. One feminine being was elevated in back of Jesus and embraced His head. Each of the other two held an arm. Two masculine beings knelt, one on either side and embraced His waist. I being left, lay at his feet, embraced his ankles, and wept for joy as I poured out my heart, like hot liquid love to my Creator and Savior. I had thought that I loved Him with all my heart, soul, mind and strength, but He showed me that my love for Him was like a drop of water in a canyon. I was astounded, but I reasoned that if Jesus appeared to me, there must be some hope for me. In turn, His love far exceeded my capacity for love. Then I said, "In this there is no satisfaction; I must do more than love God. I must worship, honor, adore, and reverence Him as what is due the Creator from a creature.

When I realized that my love could not satisfy God's capacity for love, and that his love was infinitely more than I could contain, I then wondered when and where love would be satisfied.

A few weeks later I saw and felt the presence of an angel who was among some peach trees. This angel appeared to my spirit while my physical eyes were still wide open. I didn't know at the time, but this angel was sent to prepare me for visits to Heaven. The angel said that in Heaven everyone loves everyone. This statement was rather shocking because all I knew was earthly marriage, where to be right and proper, you love only one person. But the angel continued to explain that Heaven's love is far better, far more lasting and far more delightful than the love earth understands. Heaven's love comes from God and gives perfect eternal peace. It brings uplifting, delightful satisfaction to those who help others and thus show their love to everyone. There is no law against the love that God, by His Spirit, sheds abroad in willing hearts.

The mild rebuke of this angelic exhortation caused me to despise my likeness to the animal creation, lament my ignorance of love, and desire more of the eternal love that unites and delights the saints in Heaven. I began to understand why my love for Jesus was so small.

And I prayed the Lord would evermore give me that sacred love whereby He loves His Bride the Church.

Chapter 2

MY FIRST VISIT TO HEAVEN

Shortly after this experience, while I was painting a house, three angels came and took my spirit on my first visit to Heaven. We were there instantly. Since that time, the "peach-tree angel" has taken me on many guided tours of Heaven, showing to me and describing to me its scenes and activities. I am learning that I cannot rest my soul's desires on a temporary existence in a body of death and a world of lust, because they must, and will be changed. True reality is found only in the eternal City of Heaven where my never-dying spirit experiences ecstasies pure and eternal.

After the angel showed me many things about Heaven, the Spirit of God began to show me things of a more sacred nature in the Holy City of God.

Many have questioned me about my visits to Heaven -- how I got there, and how they can get there. So here, briefly, is my understanding of how this works. The Breath God breathed into Adam at creation was God's Spirit, and Adam came to life as a body containing a soul, a spirit and the Holy Spirit. These spirits all occupy the same space at the same time in a human body, therefore Adam appeared as one person.

When I visit Heaven, my spirit and an angel visible to me are carried by God's invisible Spirit, while my body and soul (my physical nature) remain on the earth. In order to hear the call of God's Spirit, I spend much time in Bible study and prayer "watching and waiting." [Psa 130:6]

One day my spiritual eyes were opened, and I found myself in the spirit, in Paradise. There before me slightly elevated, stood Jesus, with the angel I had seen before. The reality of this place so impressed me that I said, "Surely my Dad must be here somewhere." The angel immediately replied, "Why, yes, he's right over there." My eyes followed the direction indicated, and there I dimly saw people on rows of reclining couches all of purest white. On the left side halfway back my Dad waved to me and said "Hi, son."

This scene immediately vanished and I was again standing by my Savior, close to His left hand. I was made to understand that I was slow of heart to believe all the reality of what had been revealed to me. Then the unifying Spirit of God who controls all actions in that land caused me to take Jesus' left hand and turn the palm toward me. My soul failed as I looked at the scar that doubting Thomas also saw after he said, "Except I see the print of the nails in His hands, I shall not believe." The scar, that I thought was only a little hole, was a healed tear from the base of His thumb to His two center fingers. There I saw the evidence of the precious price paid for mankind by love untold. As I beheld my Redeemer's hand, I was told, "Now you must believe," I could not restrain the tears of sorrow as I looked at the scar and realized that Jesus had to die for my sins. But thankfulness brought tears of joy because He did, and because He redeemed me, loves me, helps me understand heavenly love, and because He has prepared for me a place of perfect habitation.

Chapter 3

DIVINE PATTERN

God told Moses to build a place on earth where the people could meet to have their sins covered and learn to worship God. Moses was told to build this tabernacle like the pattern that he saw on the mount.

> *"And look that thou make them after their <u>pattern</u>, that was <u>showed thee in the mount.</u>"* Exodus 25:40

> *"And thou shalt rear up the tabernacle according to the fashion thereof which was <u>shewed thee in the mount.</u>"* Exodus 26:30

> *"(priests of earth) serve unto the example and shadow of heavenly things, as Moses was admonished of God when he was about to make the tabernacle: for, See, saith He, that thou make all things <u>according to the pattern shewed to thee in the mount.</u>"* Hebrews 8:5

✭ That pattern was, and is the City of God. So Moses' Tabernacle had a Most Holy Place within a Holy Place where the priests would serve; and around these was a large area, or Outer Court for common people. God's presence was manifested by a cloud of glory in the Most Holy Place. ✭

So also as we approach God's abode in the sky, we come first to the large Outer Court or suburbs, then to the Holy Place, then to the Most Holy Place where God sits on His Throne.

"...We have such an high priest, who is set on the right hand of the <u>throne of the Majesty in the heavens</u>. A minister of the <u>sanctuary</u>, and of the <u>true tabernacle</u>, that Yahweh pitched, and not man." Hebrews 8:1,2

"For Christ is not entered into the holy places made with hands, that are the figures of the true; <u>but into heaven itself</u>, now to appear in the Presence of God/Yahweh for us." Hebrews 9:24

In this visit we plan to see the suburbs of Heaven where we'll answer some questions including questions about sweethearts in Heaven. Then we'll enter the eastern gate, taste fruit from the Tree of Life, walk on golden streets, and experience the crystal River of Life. We plan to see the people there and how they are dressed and what they do. Then we'll tour a mansion and attend a banquet where Jesus sits at the head of the table.

We also plan to enter the Most Holy Place where God sits upon His Throne with Jesus at His right hand. In this <u>sacred Most Holy Place the saints,</u> their clothing and their Chamber Mansions are much brighter because they are closer to God on His Throne.

There are many names for Heaven in the Bible. Here are just a few: Everlasting Kingdom [Dan 4:3]--Heavenly (above the sky) Jerusalem [Heb 12:22]--High and Holy Place [Isa 57:15]--Holy Habitation [Deut 26:15]--Jerusalem that is above [Gal 4:26] --Temple of God in the sky [Rev 14:17]--The Kingdom of Heaven (sky) [Mat 3:2 & 8:11]--Throne in the sky [Rev 4:2]. We find from these names and from many other Scriptures that the City of Heaven is, and always will be, in the sky.

"It is Mt Zion on the sides of the North, the City of the Great King." Psalm 48:2

"His seed shall endure for ever, and his (David's) Throne as the sun before me. It shall be established for ever as the

moon, and as a faithful witness in Heaven." Psalm 89:36-37

*"He that walketh righteously......shall dwell on high......
You will see the King in His beauty, and behold the land
that is very far off."* Isaiah 33:15-17

*"The Lord (Yahweh) builds His stories (chambers) in the
heaven (sky)."* Amos 9:6

*"....we have a building of God, a house not made with
hands, eternal in the heavens (skies)."* II Corinthians 5:1

"....a throne was set in Heaven (the sky)." Revelation 4:2

*"The temple of God was opened in Heaven, and there was
seen in His temple, the ark of His testament...."* [temple of
God in the sky seen by men on earth] Revelation 11:19

*"And another angel came out of the temple that is in
Heaven..."* (the sky) Revelation 14:17 [also Rev 15:5 &
Rev 16:17]

*"And I saw a great white throne, and him that sat on it,
from whose face the earth and the heaven (sky) fled away..."*
Revelation 20:11

The City, where the Father will fellowship with His people forever, is always located in the sky from its creation before the world to eternity. But even on planet earth God had fellowship with our forefather Adam in Eden's Paradise. And Adam had fellowship with a sweetheart whose name was Eve. And the three of them -- God and Adam and Eve -- had a divine fellowship in that long-ago peaceful paradise that we know very little about.

But when disobedience entered that beautiful picture, God removed His indwelling Spirit from Adam and Eve. Then He took drastic measures to restore His creatures to His fellowship -- He sent Jesus, His Divine Son, to pay our death penalty. Now all who turn from disobedience (sin) and follow Jesus, will be restored to fellowship with God; and God's Spirit will return again as a dove of peace and love, to dwell in every believer.

Our relationship to the indwelling Spirit of God is like the fellowship of two friends. One friend says to the other, "Let's go to the park!" and the other friend replies, "I'm all for it. Let's go!" God's Spirit is like the first friend who knows what to do, and we are like the second friend who gets caught in the excitement of the action and the desires to go along. Jesus said:

"You will be my friends if you follow My instructions." John 15:14

We should learn this loving obedience on earth; if not, we learn it in the suburbs of Heaven where we are now going.

"If you love me, keep my commandments." John 14:15

"He that hath my commandments, and keepeth them, he it is that loveth me: and he that loveth me shall be loved of my Father, and I will love him, and will manifest myself to him." John 14:21

Chapter 4

THE OUTER SUBURBS

The City of Heaven is foursquare like a cube; [Rev 21:16] its length and width and height are each about 1500 miles. But in space, the City of Heaven appears large and round -- much larger than 1500 miles. This is because the foursquare Holy City is completely surrounded and enclosed by outer environs or suburbs. The outer edge of these suburbs is very large, making Heaven big like a planet, and, as we have previously seen, is located in the sky, forever. But the City of Heaven shines much brighter than a planet; even the righteous shine brightly.

"He built His sanctuary in the high heavens, like the earth that He established for ever." Psalm 78:69

"Then will the righteous shine brightly like the sun in the Kingdom of their Father. If your ears can hear -- hear this." Matthew 13:43

The City of Heaven with its suburbs, its Holy Place and its Most Holy Place is much larger than earth, and it is self sufficient in every way to provide for eternal spiritual beings, just as the earth is able to sustain physical life.

"And as we have borne the image of the earthy, we shall also bear the image of the Heavenly......flesh and blood cannot inherit the kingdom of God; neither doth corruption inherit

incorruption" I Corinthians 15:49-50

"My God shall supply all your need according to His riches in glory by Christ Jesus." Philippians 4:19

Now these suburbs of the City of Heaven are somewhat like earth, with grass, flowers, trees, birds and animals. This is the place where spiritual principles must be learned by those saints who on earth did not become very spiritually minded. It is not true that we suddenly know everything when we get to Heaven. Christians on earth are admonished by Scripture,

"Study to show yourself approved of God." 2 Timothy 2:15

In these suburbs or outer environs, is where saints first arrive when they come from the earth; and in this transition from earth to Heaven, they learn many things. First, they learn that they can still see, hear, smell, taste, touch and remember, and that they have a form like their earth body. This form is their spirit now out of their body. When saints leave their bodies on earth, they have a sense of freedom as birds flying. They find their thoughts to be clear and their vision able to see both physical and spiritual realms.

Some saints arriving in these suburbs would like to stay right here, but they are encouraged to move on to higher glories. And speaking of travel; it is possible in Heaven to go from place to place instantly, by taking thought. But it is more interesting and enlightening to travel slowly and enjoy the scenery. There are two methods of slow travel:

1: We can move through the air as gracefully as a white dove in the sky of earth. Most slow travel is done in this manner.

2: Some visitors to Heaven have called its vehicles by the exciting name of chariots. That's all right, but what I have seen are just seats with no flaming horses or wheels; and they are not so elaborate as to call attention to themselves. They just serve their purpose and then disappear. These chariots come in all sizes beginning with a double open-air seat for two companions, up to large bus-type open-air chariots with many double seats.

These chariots travel on land, on water or in the air, and this is how they are moved: God's Spirit harmonizes all the activities in Heaven, deciding when and where the action is to be.

When the saints hear the call of God's indwelling Spirit, their emotions respond with a joyful desire to go, and the controlling Spirit of God moves the chariot in which they ride.

In order for the Kingdom of God (it is also called the Throne of God) to be seen in the sky, it has to be a very large place.   A n d speaking of size, Jesus said to His followers:

"Which of you by taking thought can add one cubit to his stature?" Matthew 6:27

The answer, of course, was that they could not, and therefore should not worry about tomorrow. But Jesus was revealing a secret that in Heaven we can by thought, add one cubit to our height. In my visits to Heaven I noticed that people appeared to be about five feet tall. On earth a cubit is 18 inches, but a heavenly cubit is 21 inches. So a person in Heaven three cubits tall would be 63 inches, or a little over five feet tall. But when it is their turn to worship God before His Throne, they add one 21-inch cubit to their stature, making them seven feet tall.

Chapter 5

A SPIRITUAL PRINCIPLE

Now as the saints on their heavenly journey pause in these suburbs to learn spiritual realities, they are being prepared to understand and enjoy what they will experience in the Holy City. One thing they learn is the difference between physical saints on earth and spiritual saints in Heaven. And learning this will also enhance our visit.

> *"The first man, Adam, was made of dust, the second man is the Lord from Heaven. Now just as Adam was made of dust, so are his descendants. But those who are spiritual are like Jesus who is in Heaven. And as we have lived on earth like Adam in a body of dust, we shall also live in Heaven like Jesus in a spiritual body."* 1 Corinthians 15:47-49

God made us in three parts: spirit, soul and body, but the real person (the real me) is my soul. My mind, my heart, my memory, my emotions, my reasoning power -- these are the real me. These are my soul, my real person, invisible and eternal. My soul is shaped just like my body and fits into it perfectly just as a hand fits into a glove.

God gave us a spirit so we could know Him and live on a higher level than animals. But because of Adam's disobedience there is sin upon every soul, ingrained in every personality; and the only way of escape is by asking Jesus to remove our sins, save us from eternal punishment, and redeem us to eternal life with Him in Heaven.

A sinful soul uses the body for satisfaction in temporal sinful pleasures. But a redeemed soul, being delivered from ingrained sin, is united with the spirit; and while enjoying the things of God in this life, looks forward to spiritual pleasures in eternal heavenly bliss.

"To be bodily minded is death, to be spiritually minded is life and peace." Romans 8:6

A redeemed soul and spirit occupy the same space at the same time in the body, or out of the body, and in Heaven they appear as one spirit person. Spirits in Heaven have no infirmities and no signs of age, but they are recognized as the same person who lived in the body of dust, on earth. After this body of dust is resurrected and changed, the saints will live in Heaven in a glorified body like Jesus.

"(Jesus) was transfigured before them: and His face did shine as the the sun, and His raiment was white as the light." Matthew 17:2

"...we shall be like Him; for we shall see him as He is." I John 3:2

One day as I wondered what the reward would be that is promised to those who are faithful, I was taken in vision to a large treasury room, that I learned later was in the lower level of my mansion. In this room were large bins about 2 feet wide, 2 feet deep, and 4 feet long, each filled with one kind of jewel. When I saw these treasures I exclaimed to the angel who was my guide, "Are these all mine, and how did I earn all this?" I was told that God generously rewards his saints for even the smallest acts of kindness. (H F B, 6 :10)

"And whosoever shall give to drink to one of these little ones a cup of cold water only in the name of a disciple, verily I say to you, he shall in no wise lose his reward." Matthew 10:42

So knowing that rubies are among the most precious stones, I hurried with excitement to that bin and scooped up a double handful. As I playfully let them slide through my fingers back into the bin, the attending angel said, "Would you be satisfied with these as a reward? These jewels, though precious and sparkling, cannot return to you the affection you bestow on them." The realization dawned on me as the last few rubies slipped through my fingers. I knew it would take more than that to satisfy my soul.

God says, "I am thy shield, and thy exceeding great reward." (Genesis 15:1) This caused me to wonder how God could be my reward when I remembered how His love overflowed my little cup. Over time I began to understand some of the ways that God becomes my exceeding great reward -- by living in me and giving me the ability to love and enjoy the things He has created, and to love and enjoy a perfect companion.

> *"If we love one another, God dwells in us and his love is perfected in us."* I John 4:12

Realizing that my love could be satisfied, I wondered when God would be satisfied. So I said to the LORD, "To my finite way of thinking you should also find satisfaction." And He replied, "Yes, my son, He shall see of the travail of His soul, and **shall** be satisfied." (Isaiah 53:11) When My redeemed ones gather before Me on the sea of glass to worship and adore Me, with all their heart and soul and mind and strength, then will be returned to Me the equivalent of the price I paid for them on Calvary." Continuing, He said, "But the love of God goes far beyond anything that can be returned by all His creation."

Chapter 6

A BEAUTIFUL SECRET

And now I have saved this next part till the last thing before we come to the eastern gate, because I know that when you hear this beautiful secret about Heaven, you will do all within your power to make your final abode in that land of endless day.

"The secret of the Lord is with those who fear Him, and He will show them His covenant." Psalm 25:14

The secret covenant of God simply stated is eternal companionship. Consider that when God created this earth, He put two sinless companions in a perfect paradise and had divine fellowship with them. Companions in paradise with the fellowship of their Creator is therefore God's perfect will, because God called this creation good and then He blessed it.

Yes, Adam and Eve sinned and lost their covering of light, but an animal was slain so that its skins could cover their bodies. This slain animal also temporarily paid their death penalty by the shedding of its blood, until Jesus became the supreme Sacrifice for sins. Adam and Eve are now companions in Heaven by an eternal covenant.

Notice also that in Mat 9:15 Jesus calls Himself the Bridegroom and that He came to earth to purchase for Himself an eternal companion by giving His life and His blood. [Eph 5:25]

There are some remarkable comparisons between Adam and Jesus:

1: Adam is a representation of Christ. Eve is representative of the Church, the Bride of Christ.

2: God's design was for them to live in paradise and commune with Him. Jesus and His Bride the Church, will live in Heaven's paradise forever in God's presence.

3: When Adam saw that Eve had eaten of the forbidden fruit, he chose to partake also. His deep love for her, made him willing to suffer the consequences with her, rather than to be separated from her. Jesus chose to become sin for us, and suffer the consequences of death, so that His Bride could be with Him.

4: Adam was put to sleep and Eve was formed out of a rib from his side. Jesus fell asleep (died) on the cross, and from His side flowed the blood that cleanses the sin from those who will be the Bride of Christ.

When God took Eve from Adam He took more than a body of flesh and bone. He also took feminine characteristics, feminine mentality, and feminine emotions. Now, there is a vacancy in man that is only filled by God, but there is also a vacancy in a man that is only filled by the companionship of feminine characteristics, feminine mentality, and feminine emotions. God instituted companionship -- not just marriage. And this companionship is to be eternal, because there was no death when God gave Eve to Adam.

"For a man is the image and glory of God, but the woman is the glory of the man." I Corinthians 11:7

As we learn to know God who is Spirit, and invisible, we will come to understand that spiritual realm where all is perfection and wherein we will meet our perfect companion, the fulfillment of our heart's deepest desire. Our souls can never be satisfied with anything less than perfection.

We may obtain earthly riches and possessions before yielding obedience to God; but we must realize our deepest need and surrender our life to God, being indwelled by Him, before we will understand that spiritual realm of perfection where covenant companions meet.

> *"The natural man receives not the things of the Spirit of God: they are foolishness to him: neither can he know them, because they are spiritually discerned."* I Cor 2:14

Chapter 7

COMPANIONSHIP
IN HEAVEN

Adam and Jesus are not the only ones who will have eternal companions in Heaven, because fellowship and companionship is the purpose of this creation. You see, when God made Eve for Adam, it was not as though He made another apple. It was as though He cut one apple in half (sex means to divide). Adam was divided into two beings -- one masculine, and one feminine. This division was not just in the physical realm; it was also in the spiritual, mental and emotional realms. That's why a strictly physical relationship on earth does not fully satisfy the desire of men and women for companionship. There must be a relationship not affected by time or space or death -- a relationship that unites two souls, two minds and two hearts.

Now let's consider further.

"Jesus said unto them, the children of this world marry, and are given in marriage; But those who shall be accounted worthy to obtain that world, and the resurrection from the dead neither marry, nor are given in marriage: neither can they die anymore; for they are equal unto the angels; and are the children of God, being the children of the resurrection."
Luke 20:34-38

"THE CHILDREN (men and women) OF THIS WORLD

MARRY and are given in marriage. . ."

God told Adam and Eve in Genesis 1:28 to be fruitful and multiply and fill the earth. That is one God-given purpose for marriage here on earth where physical bodies grow old and die. In fact, a passage in Galatians indicates that there will not be male and female, (or the ability to reproduce), in the next world.

> *"There is neither Jew nor Greek, there is neither bond nor free, there is neither male nor female: for you are all one in Christ Jesus"* Galatians 3:28

In Heaven we are all one in Christ, we are immortal and do not die. Although these passages clearly indicate that the relationship between men and women will be different in the eternal world from what it is now, the fact that a man and a woman are united in God is plainly stated in I Cor 11:1-15 where we have the Divine order of headship.

> *"But I would have you know, that the head of every man is Christ; and the head of the woman is the man, and the head of Christ is God....Neither was the man created for the woman; but the woman for the man. For this cause ought the woman to have power on her head because of the angels."* I Corinthians 11:3, 9, 10

In other words, the divine order of headship is this: God ~ Christ ~ Man ~ Woman ~ Angels. This order is not always in effect in this world because angels are not always acknowledged, and Christ is not the head of all homes and men. Therefore we conclude that since God, Christ, Men, Women and Angels are eternal beings, that this divine order of headship will be fully in effect in God's eternity. And, lest the union of man and woman be not clear the Scripture continues:

> *"Nevertheless neither is the man without the woman, neither the woman without the man, in the Lord."* I Corinthians 11:11

> *"But THE CHIIDREN (men and women) OF THE RESURRECTION ... DO NOT DIE."*

They are eternal, spiritual beings like angels. Only they are more than angels. They are sons and daughters of God. Jesus did not cancel companionship in Heaven, He is simply explaining that resurrected beings who do not die, do not reproduce. And just like the tabernacle was a copy of the true, so earthly marriage foreshadows a future, permanent, greater union in Heaven between spiritual beings, masculine and feminine.

> "Husbands love your wives even as Christ also loved the church and gave Himself for it.... that He might present it to Himself a glorious church.... For we are members of His body, of _His flesh and of His bones_..... This is a great mystery: but I speak concerning Christ and the Church."
> Eph 5:25-32

On this earth, a feminine being lives in a female body which is flesh and blood and physical and temporary. In Heaven she lives in an eternal spiritual body. She is still feminine and looks like a lady, but she is no longer female. Spiritual glorified bodies do not have reproductive organs, because flesh and blood do not enter Heaven. The same is true for a man. In Heaven he lives in a spiritual body. He still looks like a man, and he is still masculine, but he is no longer male.

Yes, there are relationships between a man and a lady in Heaven, but there we live in glorified bodies, not physical bodies. And only in God's house will companions finally be together forever. I Corinthians tells us that the woman originally came from man. [I Cor 11:8] (as Eve from Adam)

> "This is what the Lord says...In My House, and within My walls, a place and a name ...of sons, and of daughters."
> Isaiah 56:4-5

> "In the Lord, the man and the woman are not independent of each other." l Corinthians 11:11

> "I will receive you, and will be a Father unto you, and you will be My sons and daughters, says the Lord Almighty..."
> II Corinthians 6:18

Now consider these six facts:

1: Jesus paid the supreme price to obtain a bride.

2: When God made Eve for Adam, He instituted eternal companionship, because there was no death at that time.

3: The masculine is not complete without the feminine, because in Adam they were created as one.

4: Every child born to Adam's race is only half of a perfect one.

5: Love is eternal.

6: Everyone of us, just like Jesus, desires an eternal companion.

Therefore, just as God made food for hungry bodies, and air for birds to fly in, so He has made Paradise for sweethearts.

BUT THE ONLY WAY TO THAT PARADISE IS JESUS -- THE WAY, THE TRUTH AND THE LIFE (John 14:6).

This vision of Jesus was photographed by Prince Adolph Frederick Wilhelm Von Hapsburg, the 15-year old grandson of the late Emperor of Austria. It was taken June 1, 1960 as the LORD appeared to all in the hall of Chichen Itza in the Yucatan Mission of Mexico.

Mat 28:20 I AM with you always.

John 5:43 I AM come in My Father's Name

John 6:51 I AM the Living Bread from Heaven

John 7:29 I AM from Him (the Father)

John 8:12 I AM the Light of the World

John 8:23 I AM from above

John 8:23 I AM not of this world

John 8:58 Before Abraham was, I AM

John 10:7   I AM the door of the sheep

John 10:14 I AM the Good Shepherd

John 11:25 I AM the Resurrection and the Life

Rev 1:8   I AM Alpha and Omega

Rev 1:18   I AM alive for evermore.

Rev 2:23   I AM He who searches minds and hearts

The Bible gives us a hope and a promise of eternal life beyond the grave.

"And these shall go away into everlasting punishment but the righteous into life eternal." Matthew 25:46

"My sheep hear my voice, and I know them, and they follow me: And I give to them eternal life: and they shall never perish..." John 10:27, 28

"And this is life eternal, that they might know Thee, the only true God, and Jesus Christ whom thou hast sent." John 17:3

"In hope of eternal life, that God, that cannot lie, promised before the world began." Titus 1:2

"Keep yourselves in the love of God, looking for the mercy of our Lord Jesus Christ unto eternal life." Jude 21

The Bible also gives us a hope of everlasting love beyond the grave.

"The Lord has appeared of old to me, saying Yea, I have loved thee with an everlasting love..." Jeremiah 31:3

"And hope maketh not ashamed; because the love of God is shed abroad in our hearts by the Holy Ghost that is given to us." Romans 5:5

Prophecies will end, tongues will cease, and knowledge will vanish away, but love will never die.(paraphrase) I Corinthians 13:8

God is love and God is eternal. I John 4:8 Deuteronomy 33:27

Chapter 8

QUESTIONS ANSWERED

Now your questions:

Q: Will a person who remained single on earth have a companion in Heaven?

A: Yes. Just as God chose Eve for Adam, so He will choose companions in Heaven. Jesus was not married on earth, but Rev 19:1-9 records His marriage in Heaven.

Q: Will my spouse on earth be my companion in Heaven?

A: Many married Christians have a companionship that includes mental, emotional and spiritualsatisfaction. They share a love that distance cannot hinder, time cannot diminish, and death cannot finish. And since their life on earth is a happy one, they desire to be together in Heaven, and I believe God will grant their desire. On the other hand, many marriages are unhappy, but don't let an unhappy marriage turn you against the covenant companion concept. God made for Adam a companion he would not part with; and He knows how to choose the perfectly satisfying companion in Heaven for every saved child of Adam's race. If we keep His rules here, He will keep His promises there.

The earthly covenant of marriage is till death do us part. If a partner dies, the spouse is free both legally by man's law, and God's law to marry again. If a person on earth can have more than one spouse because of death, then surely after death when we get to Heaven, God knows who the perfect companion is for us, because He is the one who created you to be one. So everyone who is married on earth is not necessarily married to their covenant companion. Many people remarry after the death of a spouse, meaning they have had two spouses, but in Heaven they only have one companion. God created you and knows you best, and knows who He created to be your perfect companion. In Heaven all will be made right.

Q: If there is no marriage in Heaven, how do companions express love?

A: A biological response is not love; it is only an expression of love, as your question has said. But God had to make it one of the physical intimacies on earth, or the race would not continue. In Heaven there are seven intimacies, but they are spiritual, and any one of them would make the earthly relationship seem like a bad dream by comparison. Eternal intimacies will be explained in the Holy City where we will soon be going. But following is a brief introduction.

☆ Spirits look like people, but two of them can occupy the same space at the same time and appear as one. This is why a soul and a spirit can both live in the same body; they are being intimate with each other and with that body. The fear of death is proof that souls and spirits are very delighted with life in a body.

"For as the body without the spirit is dead, so faith without

40

works is dead also." James 2:26

Covenant companions in Heaven (those united by God) will live in spiritual glorified bodies and so will also be able to occupy the same space at the same time, the masculine and the feminine appearing as one glorified being, united as two voices singing one duet. There is <u>nothing</u> on earth that even compares to the lasting ecstasy of this intimacy.

God's Spirit and my spirit are also delighted to be together as one in my body, because when I dedicated my life to God, I was so happy that for hours I could not speak for laughing. And this spiritual intimacy will continue forever in my glorified body in Heaven.

The Lord is intimate with the upright. (Proverbs 3:32)

"If anyone loves Me, he will keep My words; and My Father will love him, and we will come and dwell (remain) with him" John 14:23

A happy relationship with God's indwelling Spirit is required before anyone enters the gate of the Holy City.

"If the Spirit of Him that raised up Jesus from the dead dwell in you, He ....shall also quicken your mortal bodies by His Spirit that dwelleth in you." Romans 8:11

"And he that keeps his commandments dwells in him, and he in him. And hereby we know that he abideth in us, by the Spirit that he hath given us." I John 3:24

Chapter 9

THROUGH THE GATES

We are ready now to approach the eternal City of God. And we will be seeing things that are very large and very different, things that are very intricate, detailed and beautiful, and hard to describe. But I will do my best, with the Lord's help, to describe these things for you, as did St. John in Rev 21 and 22.

This City built by God is our Father's House, a very moving sight for the redeemed to behold, not only because of its bright beauty, but because of its emotional effect on those who are sincere about their relationship to Jesus, and who want to be with Him in this, His Father's House.

(Many of us have loved ones there whose love beckons us to come Home. It's my eternal Home. I have loved ones, mansions and treasures there, and I would like to stay there, but God has asked me to tell you about it.)

St. John described the wall of this City as "great and high," and because we are near, it appears to reach up out of sight. In the eastern wall, facing us, there are three gates. Each one is surrounded by huge multicolored arches having the appearance of stained glass windows. The twelve foundations are covered with precious stones of twelve different colors -- one color of gem for each foundation. The colors are so arranged that the City appears sometimes to be sitting on a rainbow and sometimes to be surrounded by it.

When we talk and sing about the eastern gate, we are referring to the center gate in this eastern wall of the City of God. This gate is important because as God and Jesus sit upon the Throne of Heaven, they face the inside of this eastern gate

It is also through this eastern gate that Jesus will lead the raptured saints into the Holy City to eat from the Tree of Life, to feast at the marriage supper of the Lamb, and to spend eternity ruling and reigning with Him.

When the raptured saints come in sight of this magnificent City and that beckoning eastern gate, and when the glorious spiritual reality of our eternal Home dawns upon our glorified sight, we will be so filled with divine ecstasy that we will shout hallelujahs and praises to God like we never knew could come from our innermost being.

It will be the heavenly fulfillment of what happened when Jesus rode triumphantly into the earthly city of Jerusalem. On earth He was rejected, but in Heaven we will all be received.

St. John said each gate was a pearl and all twelve gates are never shut. A pearl is milk-white and translucent; we can see into a pearl, but we cannot see through it. The heavenly Throne of God and of Jesus has also a bright white semi-transparent appearance like a pearl. The gates are like pearls because they are concentrated white light. [Revelation 21:21] We can see into this light but we cannot see through it. We can, however, pass through this gate of pearly light. That's why it is said to be never shut. But it does not stand open as a door on earth stands open. (Jesus on earth passed through closed doors in His glorified body.)

After we enter through the gate of pearly-white light, we see a huge hallway. With its high vaulted ceilings and wide corridor, it is about 216 feet long, because the wall of this City is 216 feet thick. There are no lighting fixtures here. The light comes from the Throne of God and begins as very bright white light.

"The sun shall be no more thy light by day; neither for

43

brightness shall the moon give light to thee; but Yahweh shall be unto thee an everlasting light, and thy God thy glory." Isaiah 60:19

"And the City had no need of the sun, neither of the moon, to shine it it: for the glory of God did lighten it, and the Lamb is the light thereof." Revelation 21:23

Then, as this light is diffused through, and reflected from, the gem-like structure of this City, there emerges a rainbow spectrum which is the blending of five major colors: gold, blue, purple, red and green.

So we see that the rainbow effect is not only in the twelve foundations, but throughout the entire City, with the first color, gold, being predominant much of the time.

*"And above the firmament that was over their (four living beings) heads was the likeness of a throne, as the appearance of a sapphire stone; and upon the likeness of the throne was the likeness as the appearance of a man above upon it......
and it had brightness round about. As the appearance of the bow that is in the cloud in the day of rain, so was the appearance of the brightness round about. This was the appearance of the likeness of the glory of Yahweh."* Ezekiel 1:26-28

The arches to your left and right, shaped like one-third of a circle, or like a rainbow, lead to rooms that on earth would be called business offices. Here the angel who keeps the gate has on record the name, the spiritual status and the works of every saint of God. In this hallway we are greeted by the angel of the gate with a joyful welcome because he knows who we are and because the angels bring only those who are worthy to enter this City. Inside this gate is one of the places where Jesus welcomes His people.

Chapter 10

INTO THE CITY

In front of us now is the area of the City called Paradise at the Father's right hand, the Holy Place and the outer court. Here we see the golden streets, the Tree of Life and the River of Life. The Tree of Life is a row of trees on both sides of the river and these trees produce twelve kinds of fruit, one for each month of the year. [Revelation 22:2] But there is more than one kind of fruit ripe at one time. One fruit given to visitors to taste, is shaped like a pear, tastes like a soft ripe peach and is so juicy that its juice will run down your arms and drip off your elbows. (Before an Old Testament priest entered the Tabernacle to serve the Lord, he had to wash his hands; and, to make sure he used enough water, it had to run down his arms and drip off his elbows.) But don't worry, the juice from heavenly fruit dries quickly and does not stain your beautiful garments.

The rows of the Tree of Life are always filled with fruit. The faster it is used, the faster it reappears; and what is left of the core then disappears. The trees are always filled with blossoms and fruit at the same time. These blossoms have a delightful fragrance that fills the air and blesses the saints who gather there.

Companions in Heaven spend many happy hours in this park talking, singing and laughing. In fact, there is always someone nearby who is laughing heartily. We each take our turn expressing our love and delight with laughter as we enjoy the tasty fruit and the colorful fragrant flowers, or as we wade, walk and play in the mile-wide river.

One day my angel guide said, "Today we're going to step into the crystal River of Life."

I said, "But I have shoes on."

Then I looked at my feet and they had no shoes on. My feet never came to my attention before in my heavenly visits; I just supposed I had shoes on. Perhaps it is because we wear them all the time on earth, or perhaps it is because of an old song about people putting on shoes and walking all over God's Heaven. I don't think we wear shoes in Heaven and I know we don't walk -- we move gracefully as on roller skates without bouncing up and down.

So we stepped into the river and the experience was very stimulating and exciting. It was my first experience in touching the water of the River of Heaven.

This crystal River of Life is not cold and wet like earthly water. We can breathe under the surface because this water is a manifestation or appearing of the Spirit of God. Walking in this river is walking in the Spirit, and these waters remove the scars and memories of sin from the souls and minds of the saints whose home is in Heaven. The sins themselves, of course, must be removed on earth by the blood Jesus shed on earth.

"Jesus ... gave Himself for us that He might redeem us and purify us from all iniquity, and make us His very own people." Titus 2:14

(God's Son) "In whom we have redemption through his blood, even the forgiveness of sins." Colossians 1:14

"Now the God of peace, that brought again from the dead our Lord Jesus, that great shepherd of the sheep, through the blood of the everlasting covenant, Make you perfect in every good work to do his will..." Hebrews 13:20-21

"...Unto him that loved us, and washed us from our sins in his own blood." Revelation 1:5

The golden streets are on both sides of the river. Close to the water, they begin to slope downward and continue under the water forming the river bed. The golden streets are clear, but they look golden because they reflect the predominant gold color of the City. Here again the effect is like pearl -- we can see into the street but we cannot see through it. The river also is clear but it sparkles more like silver. The streets are on both sides of the river and are each about 90 feet wide. In the center of each street is a 30-foot wide green lawn with a row of trees, something like a boulevard. The lawn is made of short thick grass growing up out of white sand. There are also beds of fragrant colorful flowers artistically designed and arranged. This park of trees, streets and river makes twelve spirals around and from the center of the City outward to the eastern gate. This park is about 26,000 miles long and could easily accommodate 144 million people. But in all my visits to this place, there appear to be very few people here.

Some have wondered about family circles in Heaven. Togetherness here is different than it was on earth, because, even those who had no family on earth have a companion here, from whom they never part. We do at times have a banquet in our mansion for friends and relatives but they all bring their companions. And when we attend other banquets, we go as companions. For as Eden was made an eternal paradise for Adam and Eve until they fell, so Heaven was made for companions who are restored from the fall by Jesus, to be eternal sweethearts.

There are no families here as there are on earth. But in a spiritual sense, those who are here are all one family in our Heavenly Father's big House. We can communicate by thought; but since we can't listen and talk to everybody at once, most human fellowship in Heaven is between companions.

There are also small groups of companions talking, you could say, all at once. And there are larger groups listening to an interesting person, and there are also congregations listening to platform presentations or watching video scenes.

Chapter 11

GARMENTS OF HEAVEN

There are three different garments here: the garment of humility; the robe of righteousness; and the garment of praise. To be fully dressed, we put them on in that order. Here in this paradise area between the suburbs and the Most Holy Place, the bodies of saints are completely covered with permanent white light. The body may be a spirit body or a glorified body, in either case it is white. Since I was accustomed to the pigskin color of earth beings, I thought white was rather dull. But they told me I would learn to appreciate their white soft opaque appearance -- and I did. But there is color to their hair, eyes and lips.

> Bless the LORD, o my soul, O LORD my God, thou art very great; thou art clothed with honor and majesty. Who coverest thyself with light as with a garment.....Psalm 104:1,2

The first garment covering this body of soft white light is the garment of humility. [I Peter 5:5] It is long and white, looks like opaque soft velvet and fits very neatly because it is tailored to fit. This garment of humility is for everyday use around the mansion and for performing humble service. It is also called the robe (or garment) of salvation.

Then there is a shining white garment of fine linen called the robe of righteousness. It is worn over top and completely covers the garment of humility. The robe of righteousness has fullness, it also reaches down to the feet and is also neatly tailored.

> *"They shall walk with Me in <u>white</u>, for they are worthy."* Revelation 3:4

> *"I will greatly rejoice in the LORD, my soul shall be joyful in my God; for He hath clothed me with the garments of salvation, He hath covered me with the <u>robe of righteousness</u>, as a bridegroom decketh himself with ornaments, and as a bride adorneth herself with her jewels."* Isaiah 61:10

> *"And in the midst of the seven candlesticks one like unto the Son of man, clothed with a <u>garment down to the foot</u>, and girt about the paps with a golden girdle."* Revelation 1:13

Both men and ladies are dressed alike but masculine and feminine forms can be distinguished, even when they are fully dressed. This shining garment is worn for banquets, for fellowship at the Tree of Life and River of Life and for other social activities in the Holy Place.

The final garment is coat-like and sleeveless. It is worn for praise and worship activities in the Most Holy Place. It is a very beautiful gold-threaded and jewel-decorated garment. To be dressed in all the robes of Heaven speaks of salvation, righteousness and praise. These garments compare to the garments worn by Aaron the High Priest.

> *"To appoint to them that mourn in Zion, to give to them beauty for ashes, the oil of joy for mourning, <u>the garment of praise</u> for the spirit of heaviness; that they might be called trees of righteousness, the planting of The LORD that He might be glorified."* Isaiah 61:3

This drawing of an Old Testament High Priest shows how he was dressed when he went into the Most Holy Place of Moses' Tabernacle to minister before the Lord. His first garment is a white linen embroidered coat. On top of that is a blue robe with golden bells between pomegranates around the hem. Over that is a linen ephod colored blue, purple, scarlet and gold. Around his waist is a girdle. On his golden breastplate are twelve precious stones in four rows. 1: Sardius, Topaz, Carbuncle 2: Emerald, Sapphire, Diamond 3: Jacinth, Agate, Amethyst 4: Beryl, Onyx, Jasper. On his head is a Miter. In his hands is a censer filled with incense.

In Heaven we are not concerned about tomorrow because we are so happy and satisfied today, but we do mark periods of time. The days are 24 hours long and there is no night here, but there is a corresponding soft-light quiet time of about seven hours. The other 17 hours are the bright part of the day, with gold as the predominant color and blue as the next prominent color. The day begins with the "dawn," so to speak, of the brightness. During the soft-light time, companions are together in their mansions reclining, talking, singing to each other, enjoying the garden of nuts and spices, viewing audio-visual scenes of knowledge or entertainment, and other things you will learn when you come here to stay.

There is also a seven-day schedule of events, the seventh day being mostly for worship activities described later. There are twelve months in a year, 1000 years in a millennium, 7000 years in an age and seven ages or 49,000 years (or 1000 generations earthly speaking) to an age of ages.

Looking now toward the center of Paradise, we see that the land slopes gently upward as we follow the straight street leading from the eastern gate to that tall structure ahead of us. That is the Most Holy Place where God is made visible on His Throne. We'll visit there soon but, first, let's look at my City Mansion.

Chapter 12

THE CITY MANSION
(there are also dwellings in the outer environs)

This mansion is surrounded by about ten acres of land and about an acre of flower gardens. The front yard is surrounded by seven-foot-high arbors of constantly blooming flowers, and the gate is an open heart-shaped arbor, covered with large red fragrant thorn-less roses. This arbor has seats inside on the left and on the right. I have many happy memories of my visits to this place.

This mansion has three stories with a five-story tower on the front right corner. A large double door in this tower takes us into a large circular vestibule about twenty feet in diameter. To the right, a door leads to a large banquet room. To the left a door leads to a large living room or social hall. In the center is a stairway to the upper floors and a door to the kitchen and the back of the house. The backyard is a garden of spices, flowers, fruits and nuts with rose-arbor hiding places where companions fellowship together and with Jesus. On earth Jesus appeared only one place at a time. Here, Jesus appears many places at the same time.

"O Thou who dwellest in the gardens, the companions listen to Thy voice, cause me to hear it." Song of Solomon 8:13

On the second floor there is a study library, a music room containing a large piano-like instrument with three keyboards, and a large open balcony facing the garden of spices. On the third floor there are rooms for study, meditation and servants. There are saints who desire only a small place in Heaven and they are servants here and doorkeepers and caretakers. They enjoy seeing to it that fruit from the garden is picked, dried and stored with nuts and spices in preparation for a banquet.

At banquet time, the companions who own the mansion invite their guests who come as companions. Jesus sits at the head of the table while the owners of the mansion sit at the servant end of the table. We sit in seats for two people and dine and listen to Jesus tell of wonderful things we will learn and see and do in Heaven. There is a very delightful Spirit of love and communion. Platters are passed from left to right containing small delicacies like nut butter cups and dried spiced fruit. There is soft melodious music by angelic choirs while bouquets of colorful flowers fill the air with sweet fragrance.

"Praise God, the Father of our Lord Jesus Christ for His great mercy for by raising Jesus Christ from the dead, He has given us a new birth, and a living hope for an eternal inheritance that is incorruptible and undefiled and reserved for us in Heaven." 1 Peter 1:3-4

This Holy Place of Heaven is a delightful place to be, but there are far greater glories to be enjoyed by saints who seek the face of God Most High. Blessed be His Name forever!

Chapter 13

THE TEMPLE OF HEAVEN

Looking now again toward the center of Paradise, we see a majestic round tower, shining with all colors of the spectrum -- the very center of the City of Heaven. It is 300 miles across and almost a thousand miles high. In case you wonder about the huge distances of Heaven, consider that the moon is over 230,000 miles above the earth and we think nothing of this distance when we look at the moon. Likewise the large spaces (distances) of Heaven are no problem to the saints and the angels who live here.

This round tower is called the Temple of Heaven because it contains the Throne of God and of Jesus.

"The Lord is in His Holy Temple, the Lord's Throne is in Heaven." Psalm 11:4

"And the seventh angel poured out his vial into the air: and there came a great voice out of the Temple of Heaven, from the throne, saying, It is done" Revelation 16:17

The space within the tower walls is called "the Temple" or "the Most Holy Place." It is the place of the Most Holy Presence of the Most High God, the highest state of existence for a person from planet earth. Isaiah was here [Isa 6:1]. Here the devoted saints of God dwell in chambers of divine delight, and behold the face of God. These

Chamber Mansions are located in the wall that surrounds the Throne of God and of Jesus.

> *"Therefore are they before the throne of God, and serve him day and night in His temple: and he that sitteth on the throne shall dwell among them."* Revelation 7:15

The source of the light of Heaven is the brightness of the Glory of God and Jesus. This glory light causes the Throne to be so bright that it appears like earthly snow when the sun is shining on it. And this Light shines through the walls of the Temple making the chambers there a very bright place to live. Sometimes the Light is so bright that the walls seem invisible and sometimes the walls sparkle with rainbow colors, like a tower made of diamonds with light shining thru and changing slowly.

The Light of Heaven is like a golden sunrise reflected on a blue sky. In this Light, flowers, fountains and surroundings sparkle and shine with delicate rainbow hues. Heaven is a very beautiful place, and the half has not been told.

> *(King of Kings) "Who only hath immortality, dwelling in the light that no man can approach unto; whom no man hath seen nor can see; to whom be honor and power everlasting"* I Timothy 6:16

This Temple of Heaven has three gates -- North, East and South. We are heading toward the East Gate but before we get there, we come to the three Gardens of Fountains that completely surround the outside wall of the Temple, and are enclosed at the outer edge by a delicate trellis.

Some of these sparkling fountains are small and gentle and others rise to great heights. They all fall into basins made of inlaid jewels intricately designed. Each fountain and basin is different and each design is different. Again this water is not cold and wet. It is a visible presence of the Spirit of God, Who in the Bible is revealed as water and as oil, Who also took the form of a dove, a pillar of cloud by day and a pillar of fire by night. So likewise in Heaven, the Spirit of God is manifested in many ways such as fruit on the Tree of Life and water in the crystal fountains and the crystal River of Life.

56

"O taste and see that the Lord is good." Psalm 34:8

"The water that I shall give you, will be in you a well of water springing up into everlasting life." John 4:14

Chapter 14

THE TEMPLE WALL

Passing through the Gardens of Fountains, we come to the gate on the east side of the Temple. The wall of this Temple appears to be made of multicolored snowflakes, but it is actually a very substantial substance. Being 15 miles thick, there is space within this wall for millions of rooms of all shapes and sizes and descriptions, and they are designed for every purpose necessary to the operation and administration of this City.

Within this wall of the Most Holy Place there are rooms called temples of instruction where every necessary subject is taught. Here the children who for any reason died prematurely, are taught basic heavenly knowledge. Some of these children join the angelic choirs and provide music for banquets or other occasions where their music is desired. Also in these rooms, the saints are taught the knowledge of heavenly companionship. We plan to sit in and listen to the teacher in a class for children and a class for companions.

In this Temple wall there are rooms with picture screens where knowledge is presented in a three-dimensional review of important events. Your life is on record here (and that's enough to keep anyone humble). One of the events reviewed is the crucifixion of Jesus. Even in Heaven, the story of Jesus is still the sweetest story ever told. Wouldn't you like to see the story of Jesus as it really was?

Now before we enter this Temple and Most Holy Place of Heaven, let me say that it is not just another place to visit. It is very sacred, very hallowed and very different from things understood by most earth beings. If we were to consider the dimensions of existence as being numbered from one to seven, Heaven's Most Holy Place would be number seven. The Presence of God in this Temple is the highest state of human existence, and it is only for the holy people of God. It is impossible for me to describe the things of this Temple in a way that they would be understood by those who have no spiritual perception, because higher spiritual wisdom always appears foolish to those who do not want it.

> *"But the natural man receiveth not the things of the Spirit of God: for they are foolishness unto him: neither can he know them because they are spiritually discerned."* I Corinthians 2:14

> *".....Be filled with the knowledge of His will in all wisdom and spiritual understanding."* Colossians 1:9

So those who would understand what I am about to describe must be spiritually and heavenly minded. They must seek the God of Heaven and love Him with all their heart, soul, mind and strength. And be assured that those who truly seek God will find Him. Those who find the devil were not seeking God.

> *"And you shall seek me, and find me, when you search for Me with all your heart"* Jeremiah 29:13

> *"If you being evil know how to give good gifts to your children, how much more surely will your heavenly Father give His Holy Spirit to those who continue to ask Him?"* Luke 11:13

The Bible explains that The Most Holy Place of Moses' Tabernacle on earth could only be entered once a year, by the high priest, who was ceremoniously prepared and wore special clothing used for no other purpose. The Bible also tells us of a time when two of Aaron's sons offered strange fire to the LORD, that He had not commanded, in the <u>Holy Place</u>. So the LORD's Presence consumed them and they died. Their relatives took the bodies out. [Leviticus 10:1-10] Yahweh Himself said He will be treated as Holy, by those who come near Him.

> *(after Nadab and Abihu died)* *"Moses said to Aaron, This is what Yahweh spoke saying, I will be sanctified (set apart as holy) in them that come near me, and before all the people I will be glorified."* Leviticus 10:3

So surely the <u>Most Holy Place</u> of Heaven should be considered even more sacred. I'm not trying to scare you; only to let you know that Heaven's highest pleasures are not given to unsanctified triflers. They are given to those who drink of the Spirit of God as a thirsty soul drinks from a cool mountain spring. They are given to those who breathe in the Spirit of God as they would breathe in the fragrance of flowers on a cool summer evening.

> *"As the deer panteth after the water brooks, so panteth my soul after thee, O God. My soul thirsteth for God, for the living God: when shall I come and appear before God?"* Psalm 42:1, 2

The saints in Heaven's Most Holy Place also wear clothing that is different from what they wear in any other part of Heaven. They themselves are also specially prepared, but they are not limited to one visit per year, because there are Chamber Mansions located on the inside of the walls of the Temple that face into the Most Holy Place. Companion saints spend much time in these chamber homes. From these they can behold the face of God on His Throne.

Before we partake of the Lord's supper on earth, we examine ourselves lest we partake without being worthy and perhaps get sick or die [l Corinthians 11:23-33]. I trust the foregoing admonitions have helped us to examine and prepare ourselves to enter into the Lord's presence in the Temple of Heaven.

> *"Let the words of my mouth, and the meditation of my heart be acceptable in Thy sight, O Lord my Strength and my Redeemer."* Psalm 19:14

60

In Paradise, also called the Holy Place, we traveled mostly by the slow method. Here in the Temple or Most Holy Place we travel mostly by thought.

Chapter 15

THE CHILDREN'S NURSERY CLASS

We go first to the children's nursery within the wall surrounding the Most Holy Place. Here the souls of infants from earth, including premature infants, begin to realize their existence. The infants are put into classes by angels according to their scientific, musical, artistic, social, etc., abilities. Then they are taught the knowledge and skills of Heaven by very gentle and loving angels and saints. The infants and their angel teachers live in the Light of God the Father and Jesus the Lamb as this Light shines through this wall and through these rooms on its way to light the City of Heaven. Jesus said of little ones,

> *"In Heaven their angels do always behold the face of my Father who is in Heaven."* Matthew 18:10

At an appointed day the saints and angel teachers gather their graduating students to an assembly in a very large room. Here they are addressed by a masculine and a feminine being who are companions. Listen as the feminine being speaks to the children:

> "Children, we have come to you by the will of Jesus who loved us and gave Himself for us that He might bring us to His beautiful home, the Holy City of God, where you now abide.

"We are from earth as you are, and we have come here to be your spiritual parents and to adopt you as our spiritual children. God your heavenly Father is pleased to have you in His House, and you will not ever have to suffer the things of earth any more.

"Your angel teachers are instructing you in the perfect Law of Liberty, that is the Word of God. And it is to your own personal benefit that you apply yourself with all your heart, soul, mind and strength to the understanding of these principles. Let these words of God sink down deep into your intellect, emotions and will, that there they may, as seeds, grow into the fruit of the Spirit, to make you sweet, kind, gentle, loving and patient. Then you will be full of praise, worship and adoration to your Divine Creator, Redeemer, and show love to others with lots of hugs and kisses."

These orderly and obedient children take these words as permission to fellowship. So they begin to laugh and to hug and kiss one another. After a minute or so, their adopted spiritual mother says, "Children, save some hugs and kisses for your adopted parents."

Hearing this, the boys and girls flock as a cloud around their spiritual parents who delight themselves with the hugs and kisses of these darling little children with their chubby little arms and sweet innocent countenances.

After every child is hugged and kissed by both adopted parents, the children resume their orderly places. Then their spiritual father says, "Children, Jesus is coming very soon. Follow me and do as I do."

As the words "follow me" are spoken, the two parents unite as one in the intimacy of Perfection because this is the requirement for standing in the presence of God. The parent instructor now faces away from the children and toward a bright object approaching from a great distance. The parent instructor then kneels down and lays his beautiful jeweled crown in front of him. Seeing all this, the children, who are trying to follow instructions, are a little perplexed at not being able to unite as their parents did; neither do they have crowns to lay before them. So when the parent instructor kneels and raises his hands in worship, the children are relieved and happy to at least be able to kneel and raise their hands.

The approaching Light is Jesus, followed by a multitude of heavenly beings. Jesus comes into view at an elevation that enables everyone to see Him clearly. He is seated on a golden and elaborate but conveniently-sized chair. His attendants are standing on space around Him.

Jesus then says, "Let the little children come to Me."

Immediately the parent says, "Children, come to Jesus." and then he rises and proceeds up to Jesus' right hand. The children, likewise, rise up to Jesus whose smiling countenance wins their hearts. As the children are standing in a neat formation in front of Jesus, He motions to angels at His left who give each child a shining golden crown. This golden crown represents everlasting life. When each child is wearing a crown, Jesus reaches out His hands toward them causing the children to break ranks and ascend in a cloud-like formation around Him, each child wanting to hug and kiss Jesus. This scene lasts until every child is hugged and kissed and blessed by Jesus, and graduated to the next grade. Then Jesus, with His company, departs, leaving the children with the reality of a loving Savior -- and leaving the attendants of this nursery on "cloud nine," living in Heaven and living in the Spirit.

Chapter 16

A CLASS FOR COVENANT COMPANIONS

I promised you that we would visit a class where ladies and gentlemen were being instructed in the companionship of Heaven -- the eternal relationships between sweethearts in the perfect conditions of Heaven.

In some of my visits to Heaven I joined in activities there. One of these activities was teaching a class of men and ladies about the covenant companion concept. The reason I teach this class is because I learned this subject while living on earth. It is a fact of Heaven that we cannot be rewarded in Heaven for something we did not do on earth. And the things we learn in Heaven must be taught by someone who learned that subject while serving God on earth. Every spiritual subject must be learned first from Jesus Himself before we as humans can teach it. These things can be learned and taught, both on earth and in Heaven.

So one day as I stood up to teach my class, I noticed Adam and Eve in the left rear section of the auditorium; and I wondered why they came to my class. I thought surely they must know more about the covenant companion concept than I do. The Spirit of God made known to me that just as Jesus on earth followed the ordinance of water baptism, so companions in Heaven must follow the procedure of attending a covenant companion class.

Nevertheless, I felt like the man who, as the story goes, was in Heaven describing the great flood of Johnstown, Pennsylvania, when someone told him that Noah was in his audience!

We go now to a spacious auditorium with large rooms on both sides. As we face the platform we see a large group of men and ladies in the room to the left. Bright angelic beings are arranging them so that men and ladies file into their seats alternately, a lady and a man, a lady and a man, etc., until all the seats are filled. Here now is the oration:

My companion and I greet you by the grace of God our heavenly Father, who has blessed us with all spiritual blessings in heavenly places, through our Lord and Savior Jesus Christ. It is your Father's good pleasure to give you the Kingdom of Heaven. Welcome to this class, and to the knowledge of things that will make you worthy to join those who worship with exceeding joy in the Most Holy Place of God's presence. *JUDE*

Having sought the face of God and obeyed His Word, you are those who are called and chosen and faithful, and therefore privileged to attend this in depth study on the relationship of Christ and His Bride the Church, the covenant companion concept, and the intimacies of Heaven. Let's begin with some words of the apostle Paul in 1 Corinthians 11:3-11, 15

"I would like you to realize that Christ is the head of every man, and a man is the head of a woman, and God is the head of Christ. A man should not pray or prophesy with anything on his head, but a woman should have her head covered when praying or prophesying, because to have her head uncovered is as shameful as having it shaved. So if it is shameful for a woman to be shaved, let her be covered. A man should not have his head covered because he is the image and glory of God, but a woman is the glory of a man, for Adam did not originate from a woman -- the woman was taken out of the man. For man was not created for the woman's sake, but the woman was created for the man;

therefore the woman's head should be covered as a symbol of
her authority among the angels. However, in the Lord, the
man and the woman are not independent of each other. A
woman's long hair is a glory to her, for her long hair is given
to her for a covering."

We have in this passage the divine order of headship -- God, Christ, man, woman and angels. Among physical people on earth, this headship is not completely fulfilled. But in this City, everyone is spiritual and this divine order of headship is in full effect -- God, Christ, man, woman and angels. The man and woman are never independent of each other, but while their purpose on earth was physical, their purpose in Heaven is spiritual. While on earth they represented Christ and His Bride the Church, in Heaven men and women are the Bride of Christ. As Christ is in Heaven united spiritually to His Bride the Church, so the man and the woman are in Heaven united by spiritual union.

We are met here today to consider this spiritual union and the seven intimacies of eternal companions. Let's begin with the creation of Adam.

"And God said, Let us make man in our image, after our
likeness...So God created man in His own image. In the
image of God created He him, male and female created He
them." Genesis 1:26-27

Adam's body was made of dust, but Adam's life is the Breath and Spirit of God. Adam's companion was a rib from his side, chosen, created and given by God. Eve did not come by the will of Adam, but by the will of God. Eve partook of, and shares the life of Adam as the Bride partakes of and shares the life of Christ.

Adam was willing to die to be with Eve because when she ate the forbidden fruit, he ate it, too. Jesus also died that His Bride might be with Him. But the fall of man was no accident in the plan of God, because God intended that mankind obtain the knowledge of good and evil in order to be more like Him.

"And the Lord God said, Behold the man is become as one
of Us to know good and evil." Genesis 3:22

From the very beginning God intended that men and women should be very much like Him, as He has said, "in our image," "after our likeness," "as one of us."

We live now either as mortals on earth, or as spirits in Heaven, but when Jesus completes His Bride on the resurrection day, we will all have glorified bodies like His own.

"The Lord Jesus Christ...will change our body of humility, and make it like His body of glory..." Philippians 3:21

Then we will be complete -- spirit, soul and glorified body in the City of God. Then we will partake of the Life of the Spirit of God, and enjoy our place in the divine order of headship. Then the man and the woman will be companions by an eternal heavenly covenant and enjoy their companionship by seven spiritual intimacies.

Chapter 17

SEVEN SPIRITUAL INTIMACIES

(Class continues)

#1: The first intimacy is the delight enjoyed by a spiritual soul as it dwells in a glorified body and senses the delights of this Celestial City. This is the intimacy of BEING. It will be fulfilled in your glorified body, after the resurrection.

> *"May your spirit and soul and body be perfect and complete at the appearing of our Lord Jesus Christ."* I Thessalonians 5:23

#2: The second intimacy is God's Spirit united with your spirit so that you appear as one person. Of course, you would not be here without this experience, but after the resurrection you will also be one with God's Spirit in your glorified body. Because God's Spirit dwells in every person, and controls all activities in this eternal Home of the redeemed, He places His guidance so gently upon your mind that you think it is your own desire. This is the intimacy of the SPIRIT or of BAPTISM.

#3: Intimacy number three is the intimacy of WINE. It is a love feast for partaking of God's Spirit as the New Wine of Heaven.

> *"You have kept the good wine until now."* John 2:10

#4: Two illustrations will introduce intimacy number four. As you are now one with God's Spirit, and as Adam and Eve were originally together as one, so companions here can unite together, masculine and feminine as one person. After the resurrection your glorified bodies will be able to unite in the same way. This intimacy is necessary for worship in the Most Holy Place. It is called PERFECTION, an important and much used intimacy in Heaven. In this intimacy we are called Sons of God.

God made Adam and Eve from one lump of clay [Genesis 2:23]. God met with His people at the mercy seat, and this mercy seat was watched over by two cherubim, both made from one piece of gold [Exodus 37:7-8]. Christ and His Bride the Church will become one. [Ephesians 5:31-32]

A woman should not pray unless she is covered   [l Corinthians 11:5-6], and a man should not appear before the Lord empty [Deuteronomy 16:16]. In this intimacy of Perfection, both of these requirements are met; the man is filled, and the woman is covered, and the two as one are accepted to worship in God's presence.

 "In the Lord, the man and the woman are not independent of each other." I Corinthians 11:11

#5: These first four intimacies prepare you to minister in God's presence, because they produce an ecstasy so sublime that it cannot be contained. And since the expression of this ecstasy includes all your heart, soul, mind and strength, it is really worship and must be expressed to God. So intimacy number five is the intimacy of WORSHIP when united Spirit-filled companions in the Most Holy Place of Heaven, the very presence of God, lose themselves in the rapture of wonder, love and praise to their Heavenly Father!

"Now unto Him who is able to keep you from falling and to present you faultless before the presence of His glory with exceeding joy, to the only wise God our Savior, be glory and majesty, dominion and power, both now and forever." Jude 24-25

#6: After the worshipping saints have completed their expressions of love to God, they submit themselves completely to the control of the Holy Spirit, Who carries them up to the Throne where God breathes upon them. God breathed into Adam the Breath of Life. Jesus breathed on His disciples the Holy Spirit. God breathes on His saints in Heaven an exceeding great reward (everything at one time). This is the intimacy of RAPTURE.

> *"The Word of the Lord came to Abram in a vision saying, Fear not Abram, I Am your Shield and your exceeding great Reward."* Genesis 15:1

> *"O send out Thy Light and Thy Truth: let them lead me, let them bring me to Thy Holy Hill, and to Thy Tabernacles. Then will I go to the altar of God, to God my exceeding Joy."* Psalm 43:3-4

#7: The final intimacy is when companions become one in Christ and in God, the intimacy of DIVINE LIKENESS.

> *"At that day you will know that I Am in My Father, and you are in Me, and I Am in you."* John 14:20

These are the seven intimacies between covenant companions in this eternal Paradise. And this Paradise is far better than the Garden of Eden.

When you leave this room, please exit to your right. One more announcement and then you may rise and be dismissed. Your Divinely-ordained covenant companion is the lady to your right! BETTY

(End of class)

These companions knew each other before, but now they enter more completely into the fellowship of Heaven, and into a higher bliss of worship in the Most Holy Place.

From here these companions will go to the instructor's Chamber Mansion, that is also located in this wall of the Temple. This will be our next stop after a brief explanation.

"Thy word is a lamp unto my feet, and a light unto my path." Psalm 119:105

Chapter 18

ETERNAL LIFE AND REWARDS

Everyone who enters Heaven has the same eternal life, but everyone does not have the same reward. In the resurrection we are changed in substance from physical to spiritual, but we are not changed in character. All that is required to enter Heaven and obtain eternal life is to have our sins of disobedience washed away in Jesus cleansing blood.

"(Jesus) In whom we have redemption through His blood, even the forgiveness of sins." Colossians 1:14

If you want rewards and spiritual character, in Heaven, you must while on earth add to your salvation (faith), a knowledge of unseen spiritual things. You must receive God's Spirit as your trusted guide and let Him teach you about Jesus and things to come. You must put off the old nature with its evil deeds and put on a new nature, that is like Jesus. And you must follow Jesus in humble service to mankind. Saints in Heaven are different in glory, brightness and knowledge. Let me encourage you to love God with all your heart, obey His commandments and seek the face of God.

*....giving all diligence, **add to your faith** virtue.... knowledge....temperance....patience......godliness.... brotherly kindness and love.* II Peter 1:5-7

*"If you then be risen with Christ, **seek those things that
are above** where Christ sits on the right hand of God. Set
your affection (mind) on things above, not on things on the
earth."* Colossians 3:1-2

*"For as many as are led by the Spirit of God, they are the
sons of God."* Romans 8:14

*"...put off concerning the former life the old man, that is
corrupt according to the deceitful lusts; and be renewed in
the spirit of your mind and put on the new man, that in the
likeness of God, has been created in righteousness and true
holiness."* Ephesians 4:22-24

*....... Seek the LORD and His strength, seek His face
continually."* I Chronicles 16:10,11

Having a desire to know more about the eternal world and the
future of those who trust in God, I found myself in spirit upon the balcony of a large room. Before me, on the platform, sat the Son of God,
the Lord Jesus Christ, wearing glorious garments. His countenance
was serious as He sat in what seemed to be a golden swivel armchair,
in back of a one-piece banister of solid gold, rounded on top. He appeared to be about fifteen feet tall, and the angels, standing with open
books on pedestals, one on either side of Him, were about ten feet tall.

In front of the banister, on a lower level, stood ten men dressed
in long black robes, two of whom I discerned were Moses and Elijah.
The proceedings were very solemn, but I could not hear what was being said. The Judge looked at the men, and they looked at Him, and
then He smiled such a smile that it thrilled me through and through
and everyone was happy because Jesus was smiling. Then I heard the
Judge say,

*"Well done, thou good and faithful servant; thou hast been
faithful over a few things, I will make you ruler over many
things: enter thou into the joy of thy Lord."* Mat 25:21, 23

So saying, He gestured with a move of His arm to a large open door
on His right, that I could not see through. Jesus smile caused the joy
to linger as these men filed through the door indicated by Him. Ten

more men immediately proceeded in single file to the place in front of the Judge. The same serious proceedings took place and the Judge smiled as He moved His right hand toward the door on my left and said, "Well done, faithful servant, enter into the joy of thy Lord." The Judge was less happy with the accomplishments of the third group of men, but He smiled and said, "Enter into the joy of thy Lord." By this time my curiosity was so aroused that I asked the unifying Spirit of God to allow me entrance through that mysterious door.

On the other side of the door everything was bright -- their clothing, their surroundings, and their faces. It seemed as though we were outside under a bright sky. Everyone was joyfully excited as they happily greeted one another and talked of the glorious future that awaited them. That whole excited multitude seemed under perfect control, and it affected me as though everything were under control for me personally. There was no pressure of time, only calmness and certainty controlled my movements. Then I met friends and we rejoiced as we talked about the joys and beauties that surrounded us and would surround us forever.

I got the impression that the judgment was the last solemn and feared event, and that these who had gone through it looked forward to nothing but bliss. Being impressed by the Spirit that there was more to learn at the judgment proceedings, I went with another saint back to the balcony from where I had come. By this time the works of those being judged were not producing smiles on the countenance of the Judge, for those with large rewards were judged first and the Judge was sad because he could not give these a large reward also.

After a time the deeds of those being judged actually produced sadness on the face of the Judge, who should have been smiling and making everyone happy. This sadness was felt by all those who were assembled there, even as his smiles produced joy on a former occasion.

With the Spirit of God prompting us we knelt down, and reached out our hands as if to embrace a loving God. I took an attitude of meltedness as though I were pouring out to Him all my heart and soul and mind and strength for I wanted Him to be joyful. Presently He looked at us and smiled, and His smile changed the whole scene to joy. We laughed because of the joy that was in our hearts. We knew that we could not go to Him because of the circumstances, but we wanted Him to know that from our innermost being we adored Him.

Directing our attention again to the court proceedings, we noticed that those being judged had absolutely no works at all for which to be rewarded. All the works that they had done were for themselves, or done with selfish motives, for they did not do unto others as they would have others do unto them, therefore they had no works recorded, and they suffered by reason of their loss. The Judge also suffered with them for He was touched by the feeling of their sorrows, but there was nothing He could do, for they had chosen to live as they had lived. These sorrows so affected us that we asked to be dismissed and were allowed to join those who were rejoicing in their post-judgment joys.

Entering again through the door where everything was bright, we joined many other immortals participating in the presentation of awards. Everyone was dressed in shining white garments, and laughing. There was such joy at this occasion that my spirit within me began to jump for joy.

> "For other foundation can no man lay than that is laid, which is Jesus Christ. Now if any man build upon this foundation gold, silver, precious stones, wood, hay, stubble; Every man's work shall be made manifest: for the day shall declare it, because it shall be revealed by fire; and the fire shall try every man's work of what sort it is. If any man's work abide which he hath built thereupon, he shall receive a reward. If any man's work shall be burned, he shall suffer loss: but he himself shall be saved; yet so as by fire."
> 1 Corinthians 3:11-15

After the judgment of the saints, will be the marriage supper of the Lamb. It is the time when those who are redeemed and restored to fellowship with God, will be united. It is also a time when the Heavenly Bridegroom is united with His bride whom He redeemed and purchased at the price of his own life's blood. While on earth Jesus said,

> "...With desire I have desired to eat this Passover with you before I suffer: for I say unto you, I will not anymore eat thereof, until it be fulfilled in the kingdom of God...I will

not drink of the fruit of the vine until the kingdom of God shall come. " Luke 22:15-18

Jesus desired greatly to finish redemption's plan, looking forward to the time when He would rejoice over His bride:

"....As the bridegroom rejoices over the bride, so shall thy God rejoice over thee" Isaiah 62:5

"Husbands, love your wives, even as Christ also loved the church, and gave himself for it... that He might present it to Himself a glorious church, not having spot, or wrinkle, or any such thing; but that it should be holy and without blemish." Ephesians 5:25 & 27

"The Lord God omnipotent reigneth. Let us be glad and rejoice, and give honor to Him; for the marriage of the Lamb is come, and His wife has made herself ready. And to her was granted that she should be arrayed in fine linen, clean and white: for the fine linen is the righteousness of saints. And He said unto me, Write, Blessed are they who are called to the marriage supper of the Lamb.

And He said to me, These are the true sayings of God." Revelation 19:6-9

From these scriptures we find that it is one of God's desires to be united with those who love him and whom He has purchased at an unvalued price. So great is God's desire for this union with obedient created creatures that He created man as one and then separated him into two parts, masculine and feminine, ever dependent upon, and ever longing for each other, that we may in a small measure feel as he does and understand his longing and love for us. Jesus died for His beloved Bride and "greater love has no man than this". Soon now He will return and take her to be with Himself.

"I will come again, and receive you unto myself; that where I am, there you may be also." John 14:3

Chapter 19

THE CHAMBER
MANSION

In the Holy Place we saw the crystal River, the Tree of Life and the streets of gold. We saw the City Mansions, pleasant and delightful and only a little different from earth. We also saw that the saints there are a lot like people on earth, but now with a glorified body. But the mansions, beings, saints and clothing you are about to see, here in the Most Holy Place, will be very different. These saints live close to the bright Throne of God and they are dressed in light so bright that you can see them only if you are one of them. The saints who live in city mansions see the saints who live in this Temple as very bright lights. Paul tells us in I Corinthians 15 that those who rise from the dead on resurrection day, or those who remain alive and are changed in the twinkling of an eye, are as different from each other in glory and brightness as the sun, moon and stars are different from each other in earthly brightness.

"And they that be wise shall shine as the brightness of the firmament; and they that turn many to righteousness as the stars for ever and ever." Daniel 12:3

"There is one glory of the sun, and another glory of the moon, and another glory of the stars: for one star differeth from another star in glory. So also is the resurrection of the

dead. It is sown in corruption; it is raised in incorruption."
I Corinthians 15:41, 42

So now if you really desire with all your heart and soul to be near to God, come with me.

The first time I entered my Chamber mansion in the wall of the Temple, I knew not where I was. It seemed as though I was entering into a scene beyond the realm of human existence -- a scene containing objects of adornment in beauty far surpassing such familiar things as flowers, trees, clouds and rainbows. The Light in this ecstatic domain was so bright and powerful it was not stopped by my body and I had no shadow! I feared to go any further lest I be consumed by the piercing brightness of the Light.

Three different times the Spirit of God tried to show me this hallowed place but my spirit was too weak. Finally, being strengthened by the Lord, I was taken into a scene difficult to describe.

Having nothing to compare, I shall begin my description with what I call a flower. It had a stem about two feet high that resembled a clear plastic drinking straw. This was topped by a sparkling red ruby two inches in diameter. From this red ruby center there extended three "petals" fourteen inches long, made of solid shimmering diamond. These petals were one quarter of an inch in diameter where they joined the ruby center and tapered with straight sides to a needle-sharp point.

Then I noticed that everything was made of a substance like pure glass or crystal, and that each object reflected all the colors of the rainbow in a pattern all its own. Blended with these colors I heard music, and my attention was directed to a little brook of sparkling crystal water as the source of the music. As I started toward this musical water, I became conscious of a glorious rapture filling and thrilling my soul. I was blending with the surrounding atmosphere, and was in harmony with the music from the little brook. Looking through the water to the bottom of the brook, I discovered the source of the music. Precious gems were placed in symmetrical positions so that music was produced by the water flowing over them.

Suddenly I noticed two strange human-like beings as clear as glass, and I was very much startled by the presence of these "other-world"

beings. That they had not noticed me was a slight relief, so I gazed with wonder and amazement at these two strangely beautiful beings -- one masculine and one feminine. They were as smooth and transparent as clear glass, yet they appeared to reflect light like silver. They moved in unison like soldiers marching and were perfectly in place and at home in their surroundings.

Then they noticed me! And I suddenly felt as out of place as a pig in a parlor. I wanted to turn and run but the Holy Spirit, my Guide, made me face the sad fact that I was an unworthy inhabitant of this celestial abode in my present sin-marked body. But I know that someday I will have a glorified body like Jesus, and that this was a vision of my future state with my covenant companion in our chamber.

The word "Tabernacle" (a name for God's House) means "a clear shining home easily seen from a distance." So also a chamber in the Most Holy Place of Heaven is a clear shining home easily seen from a distance. This chamber is about 12 feet high, 24 feet wide and 216 feet long. The garden we first visited is toward the back of the chamber. At the front of this chamber is a living room. The walls look like soft clouds with rainbow colors upon them with ever-changing and blending hues.

There is a very large couch-like piece of furniture. It is bright white and looks like a big ball of cotton. It quickly and easily conforms to, or changes with, any sitting or reclining posture -- very comfortable.

The entire front wall is an open window. Through it we can see or enter into the Most Holy Place and its activities. This Most Holy Place is a round area about 300 miles across and about 1,000 miles high. The Throne of God and of Jesus is at the top west side, facing east. From this position the Lord can easily see all the City mansion chambers, because they adorn the face of the inside of the wall of the Temple. So also the saints in the chambers can easily see God on His Throne and Jesus at His right hand.

The chambers are in rows or stories reaching two thirds of the way around the inside of the Temple wall from the left side of the Throne to the right side of the Throne. There are 144,000 chambers in one row and 288,000 rows. Our chamber is over 800 miles above the courtyard garden and toward the left side of the Throne.

In Heaven, distance does not make things look small. Although they are earth-miles away, they seem to be magnified or enlarged as though spiritual eyes contained telescopes like the eye of an eagle.

"The entrance of Your words gives light; it gives understanding to the simple." Psalm 119:130

"It is the spirit that quickeneth; the flesh profiteth nothing; the words that I speak unto you, they are spirit, and they are life." John 6:63

Chapter 20

THE THRONE OF GOD
AND OF THE LAMB

Inside the jasper walls of the Temple or Most Holy Place is a court-yard garden. High above this enclosed garden, at the top of the beautiful walls is the Throne of God, characterized by a brilliant rainbow. This bright rainbow illumines the entire court with a perpetual profusion of prismatic hues. The space from the garden floor, to God's throne above, to the high walls round about is the seventh dimension. This hallowed habitation is the Holy of Holies of Heaven --- the very Presence of the One true God who is the Temple of Heaven and the only Light in Celestial realms. Isaiah had a vision of God's Throne, high and lifted up and His train (glorious light came down and) filled the temple [Isaiah 6:1]

No one enters this sacred abode without first receiving a desire to do so from the Spirit of God. They must be willing to suffer with Christ in this world. We are heirs of God and joint-heirs with Christ, if we suffer with Him that we may be also glorified together. [Romans 8:17]

"The sufferings of this present time are not worthy to be compared with the glory that shall be revealed in us"
Romans 8:18

The call of the Spirit to enter this sacred abode comes to those who look beyond the things of this world, and who press with heart and soul toward the high calling of God in Christ Jesus. This is the testimony of Paul the apostle who visited this Throne Room of God and called it the <u>third Heaven.</u> He said he learned things so sacred, he was not allowed to speak of them.   [II Corinthians 12:1-4]   ✗ *PARIDISE*

> *"Brethren I count not myself to have apprehended: but this one thing I do, forgetting those things that are behind, and reaching forth to those things that are before, I press toward the mark for the prize of the high calling of God in Christ Jesus."* Philippians 3:13-14

God on His Throne is the center of all things, and from God comes the Light of Life. This bright white Light makes the City of God appear brighter than the sun in the sky of earth; in fact, the day is coming soon when the City of God will appear in the sky of earth, and the brightness of this City will outshine the sun and the moon.

> *"For by Him were all things created, that are in Heaven, and that are in earth, visible and invisible, whether they be thrones, or dominions, or principalities, or powers: all things were created by Him, and for Him: And He is before all things, and BY HIM ALL THINGS CONSIST."* (everything is held together) Colossians 1:16, 17

> *(Paul)... "I saw in the way a light from Heaven, above the brightness of the sun, shining round about me..."* Acts 26:13

It would seem that being close to the throne, we would be blinded by the light. But this is not the case. Because those who are allowed to come close to God on His throne are given brighter glory and this makes it possible for them to see God. It is God Himself who chooses who comes near Him. Jesus brought the light of life to men, and made it possible for saints to enter Heaven, and dwell in the light there.

> *"Blessed is the man whom thou choosest, and causest to approach unto thee, that he may dwell in thy courts: we shall be satisfied with the goodness of thy house, even of thy*

holy temple." Psalm 65:4

*"According as he hath chosen us in him before the foundation
of the world, that we should be holy and without blame
before him in love."* Ephesians 1:4

The River of Life begins at the Throne of God. (Rev 22:1) This
River is the Spirit of God flowing from the Throne, through each
chamber in the Temple wall, then down into the fountains. This River
of Life then continues in twelve spirals around the Temple out through
the Holy Place to the eastern gate. From this gate of Heaven the River
moves as the invisible Spirit of God to bless those on earth who will
accept Him. If we walk in the Light and in the Spirit on earth, we will
walk in the Light and in the River in Heaven.

*"There is a river, whose streams shall make glad the City of
God, the Holy Place of the tabernacles of the Most High."*
Psalm 46:4

The Throne of God appears to rest on a large white-with-light oval
structure about 100 miles wide, 50 miles front to back, and 25 miles
high. But then again its size seems to vary greatly. It is difficult to
describe; you will have to see it for yourself.

In front of the Throne is a large oval area called the Sea of Glass,
paved with blue sapphire gems. [Rev 4:6] It is like a movable platform;
it disappears when not needed and its size is adjustable. (On the other
side of the Sea of Glass from the Throne is the Ark of God with the
Mercy Seat, and the Altar of Incense. (The prayers of saints are called
"incense." Rev 5:8.) When the apostle John was in this Most Holy
Place, he saw souls of martyrs under the Altar of Incense, praying God
to hasten judgment upon the earth. [Rev 6:9-10]

*"And the temple of God was opened in heaven, and there was
seen in His temple the ark of His testament: (covenant) and
there were lightnings, and voices, and thunderings, and an
earthquake, and great hail."* Revelation 11:19

At appointed times there are various methods of worship in the
space below where the Sea of Glass sometimes appears. But I find it
difficult to describe these things because of sacred secrets that some

earth dwellers who have not seen invisible things may not understand. However, I would like to describe worship activity for you as it takes place in the large area of the Most Holy Place before God's Throne. This first worship activity is called "Cup of Love."

Thousands of companion saints gather into this space before the Lord on His Throne, dressed in garments of very bright white Light. These garments are decorated with sparkling jewels in the five major colors of Heaven: gold, blue, purple, red and green. The saints place themselves in a round cup-like formation, like a large perfectly-shaped drinking glass, very artistic and beautiful. This symbolizes a vessel of honor and cup of love to Jesus who drank the bitter cup of death for these very saints who are now expressing their love to Him. Then the cup begins to turn slowly, resulting in beautiful, changing light patterns. This is the worship of love and is very delightful to God and to Jesus and to all who in this arena behold.

"He shall see of the travail of His soul, and shall be satisfied."
Isaiah 53:11

One day as I approached the Throne, there were already many people gathered on the sea of glass, who were showing their thankfulness to their Creator for their place in this delightful Home. Some were kneeling, some were standing, some reached their hands toward him, some lay on their faces before the presence of His Glory. Each in his own way was showing worship and adoration to the King of Glory, in response to an inner desire from the unifying Spirit of God. We wanted to be here more than any other place in Heaven, for our hearts burned with a desire to express our love to Jesus who expressed his love by dying in our place. In Heaven, the Spirit of God indwells everyone and causes unity, harmony and purpose throughout these vast realms of bliss and immortality.

At another time I was the only one in the great arena of space before the Throne of God. The Sea of Glass was removed and I was raptured with wonder, love and praise. In my ecstasy, I was waving my arms and dancing and spinning around, and as I did so, the five colors of Heaven were coming from the five fingers of each of my hands. I was not conscious of writing anything, but the trails of color remained in space as a love letter to God even after I finished my worship. That is when I learned about the five major colors of Heaven.

"And His brightness was as the light; (sunlight) He had horns (bright beams) coming (flashing) out of His hand, and there was the hiding of His power." Habakkuk 3:4

Chapter 21

THE FACE OF GOD

"Blessed are the pure in heart, for they shall see God."
Matthew 5:8

People have a tendency to be fearful of God because of their failures. Even some devoted saints are so afraid of God they do not seek His presence. But God does not see your failures. He sees a beloved child within the righteousness of Jesus. And God your Heavenly Father would love to have you come near to Him.

"But now in Christ Jesus ye who sometimes were far off have been brought near by the blood of Christ." Ephesians 2:13

"Let us draw near with a true heart in full assurance of faith, having our hearts sprinkled from an evil conscience, and our bodies washed with pure water." Hebrews 10:22

I stood upon the sapphire Sea of Glass with a multitude of saints all arranged in orderly fashion as Jesus presented us to God the Father. God is not an old man with hollow cheeks and long white beard, whose delight is to punish sinners. No. He loves those who seek to do His will, even though we sometimes fail; and He is drawing us to Himself by the circumstances of life. Most people just don't seek God until things get bad, so sometimes God lets things get bad so we will seek Him. If we seek Him when things go well, then He will make things go well for us so we seek Him more. To stand on the sapphire

Sea of Glass and look into the face of God is to look into the face of the One who loves you and delights to see YOU. You will never be the same after this experience. Look forward to that day with confidence.

"Anyone who will confess Me before men, that person I will also confess before My Father in Heaven." Matthew 10:32

"I love them that love Me..." Proverbs 8:17

When God sits on His Throne before a gathering of saints, He makes Himself big enough so that all may easily see Him. But when He is giving a personal interview, He appears to be, if He were standing, only twelve to eighteen feet tall. And His Throne also appears to change in size.

One day Jesus wanted to present me to His Father in Heaven. Now I knew from previous experiences that Jesus refuses to let me think that I am unworthy, because He has told us to pray that we should be considered worthy to stand with Him. So although I was a little afraid, I did want to go with Jesus to see God the Father.

"Watch therefore, and pray always, that you may be accounted worthy to escape all these things that shall come to pass, and to stand before the Son of man." Luke 21:36

Jesus said to His Father, "This friend of Mine has been wanting to see You, " -- and I looked into the face of Love! My anxiety vanished. His expression was so loving and kind that I lost all my fear, and my soul was calm. His love made me feel free, and able to love Him in return. He gave me the impression that He waited from eternity just to see me face to face. He looked like a handsome young man and Light was shining from His face. He completely ignored the fact that I am only a creature, and His manner of speech made me feel like a long-time good friend of His. Being in His presence has not only changed my idea of Him but has also changed me -- forever!

Let me share with you what I call the 'Song of the Soul'.

The Creator and Eternal One is my God. He is the Wonder of wonders to me. My finite understanding cannot comprehend His greatness. He broods over my soul like a jealous lover, lest He lose me. My name is written on His hands; I have a place in His heart dearer and more intimate than any other substance of His creation.

For me He bore the cross of shame, and shed His precious blood; for me He bears nail scars in His hands. He tore away the bars of death so that I might be united with, and embraced by, those dear unto my soul. He opened Paradise and the presence of God so that I might enter in. When I humbly confessed my sin, asked Him to forgive me and cleanse me from all unrighteousness, He made me perfect in His sight, and took away everything that would hinder me from entering the Holy City of God, where peace like a river gently flows and pure love moves from heart to heart.

He satisfies my deepest need; in Him I find all that is necessary for righteousness and godliness in this world. In Him I find all that is necessary for satisfaction and bliss in the eternal world. I will live for Him, having surrendered my soul to Him and to those things that are true, pure, just, holy, lovely, righteous, virtuous, honest and glorious.

Many things are written about Him and many things are said about him but to me it is sweeter than all to know that He loves me.

Seek His presence. Seek His face. He loves YOU, too.

"Glory ye in His holy name: let the heart of them rejoice that seek the LORD. Seek the LORD and His strength, seek His face continually." I Chronicles 16:11

"As for me, I will behold thy face in righteousness: I shall be satisfied, when I awake, with thy likeness." Psalm 17:15

One evening while fasting and praying, a vision of Jesus impressed me. I stood on the left side of the throne of Jesus, who was robed in soft garments of purple and white. In front of Him and to my left were gathered a great multitude of souls, redeemed because of Jesus' love for them. They were lovingly singing and shouting His praises. In my hands I held a beautiful crown of gold, delicately engraved and glittering. Though it was large I marveled to myself at its lightness. But it had to be large because Jesus was very large of stature so that I had to be elevated high enough to allow me to reach His head.

As I stood holding the crown I could feel in my heart that every one of my fellow creatures down there on the sea of glass before the throne were in accord with what I was doing. I deeply loved every one of them, and felt in return their deepest, warmest, truest, unrestrained love, that helped greatly to strengthen me.

With the front of the crown in my left hand, I gently placed it upon the beautiful hair of His head as a great and joyous volume of praise and adoration arose like a mighty anthem from the throng before the throne. My heart melted as I realized anew what my Savior's love means to me in making it possible for me to be here. Trying to embrace Him I could not reach around Him for He was much larger in stature than I, but He took me in His arms as reward for what I had done and to comfort me in my weakness of spirit; and also to impress upon the congregation His great love for them, and His appreciation for their act of love.

> *"Yea, He is altogether lovely. This is my beloved, and this is my friend..."* Song of Solomon 5:16

Finally, let me encourage you to be a friend of Jesus. Obey the Holy Spirit and seek the face of God. I have given my testimony in order that you may be among those of whom the Bible says:

> *"And they shall see His face and know His Name."* Revelation 22:4

One day recently as I approached the Sea of Glass before the Throne, there were many patriarchs and prophets and righteous men already gathered there to pray and to worship God on His Throne. As it says in Job 1: 6,

> *"The sons of God came to present themselves before the Lord."*

I learned that those who on earth were concerned about the souls of men, are in Heaven still concerned about things on earth. I heard the souls of martyrs under the altar and their pleading cry, "Until when, O Lord will You delay Your vengeance on the earth dwellers who shed our blood?" Their earnestness almost caused me to weep.

I spent seven days there joining the prayer and praise to God. I learned that God is consulting with His concerned servants both in Heaven and on earth, informing them that Jesus will soon appear, and the time is short.

"For the Lord Himself shall descend from Heaven with a shout, with the voice of the archangel, and with the trump of God: and the dead in Christ shall rise first: Then we who are alive and remain shall be caught up together with them in the clouds, to meet the Lord in the air: and so shall we ever be with the Lord. Wherefore comfort one another with these words." I Thessalonians 4:16-18

Chapter 22

BRIGHT CLOUDS

In order to help me understand what I was seeing in Heaven, sometimes God would perform something special for me on earth.

One Sunday morning in Florida, my family and I were sitting in church when I noticed a strange lighting effect. I looked out the window and saw a beautiful sight. The sky was covered with bright clouds lighted by the morning sun with a golden color. This produced bright golden light shining from all parts of the sky. The tree leaves were gold colored; the ground and the buildings and the bushes were all gold colored; and there were no shadows under the trees! I told my family that there are scenes like this in the Holy Place of Heaven.

One Sunday in May, as we were outside preparing for a singing engagement that evening, my daughter Joy ran excitedly out of the house and said,

"What is that strange cloud up there?"

I looked up and saw a large bright cloud, oval shaped like the Sea of Glass before God's Throne. Large clouds are usually bright around the edge and dark in the center. This cloud was extremely and evenly bright all over its surface. Close to the cloud and completely surrounding it, was a very thin black line like you see at the edge of a clear bubble where the light rays are bent together.

I said, "There is something supernatural about that cloud."

The cloud retained its brightness as it became smaller and smaller and in about fifteen minutes disappeared from sight. Immediately following this, and in another part of the sky, we saw a five-minute display as two short streaks of light formed from top to bottom, then other streaks appeared forming rungs in a ladder in the sky and then all vanished.

Pondering all this, I wondered what the Bible said about bright clouds, and then I remembered the transfiguration in Matthew 17:2-5, where Jesus gave to three of His disciples a demonstration of His coming in His Kingdom. His face shone as bright as the sun, and His clothing shone like white light, and a BRIGHT CLOUD overshadowed them.

I think the meaning of all this is that Jesus is soon coming in His Kingdom, the City of Heaven, and (He) will shine like the sun in the sky. [Mat 13:43]   (THEY)

Will you be ready to live in that beautiful City? Jesus died on the cross that you may live forever. His shed blood can wash the sins from your soul.

Pray this prayer with me:

Jesus I'm sorry for my sins

    I believe you died on the cross in my place

        Please forgive me and wash my sins away

            Teach me to pray,

                Help me to read the Bible,

                    Help me to be ready when You return,

                I ask this in Your Name, Jesus.

        Thank you, Lord, for saving my soul!

"If you shall confess with your mouth the Lord Jesus and believe in your heart that God has raised Him from the dead you shall be saved." Romans 10:9

Now read your Bible and ask the Lord to help you understand it. Ask the Lord to help you in your daily life, and thank Him for all He does for you.

PART TWO

TESTIMONY OF THE FAMILY

COMMENTS
by Mrs. Grace Hetrick (Oden's Wife)

Some years ago a dear elderly gentleman friend of ours came to visit in our home. Then as he was leaving, he expressed his appreciation and, with tears in his eyes, said to our family of seven, "It's difficult to leave; it was 'a little bit of Heaven' being with you."

We were deeply touched and have never forgotten his words, nor have we forgotten to praise the Lord many times for the blessing and encouragement they brought to our hearts.

That seemed to assure us that God was with us, and ever after, we desired to live up to that expression, little knowing what great and wonderful things the Lord had planned for us.

Oden had often shared with me the delightful heavenly experiences and insights God gave to him from time to time. As our five children grew, he told them the beautiful stories of Jesus and of the place He has gone to prepare for those who love Him.

Now as I have helped to prepare the original manuscript for this book, I have been amazed and blessed to find that our son and daughters have volunteered a "little bit of Heaven" from their own hearts. God is faithful! What a joy to be His servants!

May you, too, be blessed and lifted up into heavenly places with Christ Jesus as you read what God has so graciously made known by His Holy Spirit.

Psalm 16:11 -- Thou wilt <u>show</u> me the path of life: in Thy presence is fullness of joy; at Thy right hand there are pleasures forevermore." Jesus said, "I go to prepare a place <u>for you</u>."

DEAR ONES IN GLORY

by Sylvia Hetrick (Oden's mother)(1897-1970)

On Thursday, June 28, 1928, I was taken to the hospital in great pain three days after my mother's funeral and six weeks after the birth of my fourth child, Lewis. After a few days of examinations and consultations between six doctors, I fell into a deep coma on Saturday about noon.

It seemed I was wandering for a long time through semi-darkness and mist, through dim and dismal scenes, presently finding myself on the bank of a slowly flowing sinister-looking stream. The water appeared dark and cold and about ten or twelve feet wide. No rippling or murmurs just slow movement past me. My mind registered the thought that this must be the river Jordan and that I was dying and would have to cross over. After some hesitation, I stepped in and found it very shallow. Proceeding step by step, slowly, I felt the water rapidly becoming deeper and it was numbingly cold. It soon was washing over my lips as I neared the middle of the stream.

Dreading the thought of drowning, I stopped, and heard my name being called in loving accents. Raising my eyes, I saw the farther bank, and beyond it a lovely park-like area of grass and trees, and over all, a sort of luminous twilight. An indescribable feeling of utter peace filled my being and, raising my eyes, I beheld my smiling mother and my sister who had also passed away a few years before. They both had in this life suffered greatly, but now they radiated health and well being. Their faces shone with love and joy as they told me how glad they were to see me there. They told me that I was standing in the middle of the stream and Jesus had sent them to welcome me and help me up the bank on the other side.

I longed to go to them, but was stopped by the sound of children weeping, coming to me across the water. Turning about, I saw my four children (Oden, Frances, Bill and Lewis) on the bank I had left, reaching out their arms to me and crying "Mama, Mama!" Turning to my mother and sister, I told them how very strongly I wanted to join them but would have to return to my children. Their expressions changed instantly to sadness and regret, as they said that Jesus had told them I could return to my family provided I turned away at once and did not look back. They said that they understood and that they, being mothers, knew the compulsion that urged me to return to my family.

So I started back and, oh, the water was so deep and so cold and the current was very strong making it extremely difficult to keep my footing and go step by slow step back through the stream. I have never known any more difficult task than to go back through that stream! I could hardly proceed at all, but the thought came into my mind to just keep breathing.

After what seemed a long, long time, my strength nearly failing, the pull of the current left me. The water receded and I felt as though I were being lifted onto the bank where I sank down utterly exhausted and knew nothing until a voice called my name. I opened my eyes to see a nurse's aid standing by my bed and her kind voice asking if she should feed me my lunch.

Later, the six doctors came to my bedside again and the head surgeon spoke to me very comfortingly and very reassuringly. I didn't know that there was just one chance in three hundred that I would recover without a serious operation and that I was too weak to stand an operation, so that there was no hope for me in that direction. However, he pledged the full resources of that great hospital to help me to pull out of this. He said that there was something for me to do, too, that I was to try very hard to get well. From that day, the assurance never left me that I would recover.

After 3 more weeks in the hospital under treatment, and one year of convalescing at home -- a year of discouragement and pain, and very difficult living, the family doctor stopped by to see me and told me that I would recover without an operation. This was great news to me.

I want to say here that all the doctors and surgeons that were connected with my case gave all the glory to God. They said that their best efforts would have been of no avail without help from Him. The head surgeon said that God must have something in this life for me to accomplish that He would restore me from such a serious illness.

At the end of that year of convalescence, I was again in full stride and very active. I later had two more children (Marjorie and Sylvia) and led a very full and active life. I have felt God's strength in my body from day to day knowing that it was only through His will that I was here at all, and that He would never forsake me or leave me, as long as it was His will for me to live.

This experience is as clear to me as the time it happened. Nothing has dimmed or faded. Full assurance remains that there is a place reserved for me in Heaven. Fanny Crosby's beautiful hymn, MY SAVIOR FIRST OF ALL, has special meaning to me now, especially the third verse:

Oh, the dear ones in glory

How they beckon me to come,

And our parting at the river I recall.

Through the sweet vales of Eden

They will sing my welcome home;

But I long to see my Savior first of all!

In his childhood, Oden's mother sang this lullaby to him:

Visions of angels happy and free

Out of the twilight coming to me

While in this earthland, sadly I roam

Seeking my far off home.

Far away, beyond the starlit skies

Where the love-light never, never dies!

Gleameth a mansion, filled with delight,
Sweet, happy home, so bright.

A PATTERN OF THINGS TO COME

by David Hetrick (Oden's Son)

It was the middle of February as we returned to our Pennsylvania headquarters. Our research concerning the days of darkness, the appearing of the bright City in the sky and the coming of the Lord was fresh in our minds. We were expecting then, as we are still, that these events would occur very soon. Friday was the day we set our course northward from St. Petersburg, Florida for the last time.

That afternoon one of the fiercest storms through which we ever recall having traveled came upon us. We drove through pouring rain, claps of thunder, and ominous flashes of pink lightning. Dad even reported that eerie screaming noises were emanating from the CB radio in his vehicle.

We set up camp early that evening somewhere in northern Florida in the rain. Saturday the storm had eased some, but we pushed on through the cloudy and rainy weather till we reached our destination in Madison, Georgia. There we parked for the night near the church where we were scheduled to sing the next morning.

Sunday dawned a beautiful spring-like day. The sun shone brightly, the air was warm and the birds were singing. It was delightfully calm and peaceful -- the storm had passed. Inside the large old nineteenth-century church building, the service began. As I looked around me from the platform where I stood, I began to notice something different about the building -- something in its architectural design was quite unique. The sanctuary seemed to be square. Yes, that was it. In fact, the floor, the ceiling and the walls surrounding me were foursquare.

The room was as high as it was wide as it was long. This is very interesting indeed, I thought to myself as my curiosity caused me to investigate further. Then I saw that high in the center, the ceiling was dome-shaped. In each wall there were three tall windows with pointed arch tops. Also in each of the four walls were three double-door entrances into the sanctuary. The wall behind me had only two entrances, the platform and pulpit being in the place of a center doorway.

As I stood there marveling at that earthly pattern of the heavenly temple, I thought what a picture of things to come. After the storms of this life and the blackness of the night, we will enter into that beautiful City foursquare to worship our Lord and Savior in peace forevermore.

I had remembered seeing the steps around the outside of the church's foundation and determined to go out as soon as the service ended to see if they numbered twelve in all -- like the foundations of the Holy City.

Psalm 18:16 & 19 "He reached down from heaven and drew me out of my great trials. He rescued me from deep waters. He brought me into a large place; he delivered me because he delighted in me."

FROM MY PRAYER DIARY

by Lois Hetrick (Oden's Daughter)

I always believed visiting Heaven was both possible and proper. We read books of people who visited Heaven in the past hundred years. I read the Bible and believed what it said about "setting your affection on things above" Col 3:2, and "looking at the things that are not seen, because the things that are seen are only temporary" 2Co 4:18.

I believe that God is the "God of the living and not of the dead" Luke 20:37-38. Therefore the men and women I read about in the Bible became my friends. I knew I would meet them someday. Isaiah said, "I saw the Lord, high and lifted up and His glory filled the Temple" Isa 6:1. Daniel saw the "Ancient of Days sitting and the Son of Man being brought before Him" Dan 7:9, 13. Stephen saw "Jesus standing on the right hand of God" Acts 7:56. Peter, James and John saw Jesus, Moses and Elijah on the mountain. (Mat 17:1-3). Enoch walked with God and God took him to Heaven. (Gen 5:24) Paul said we come to the Living God, innumerable angels, the spirits of just men made perfect, and to Jesus in the Heavenly Jerusalem. (Heb 12:18-24)

Paul continues, "Jesus Christ is the same yesterday, today and forever" Heb 13:8 "we have a Great High Priest that is passed into the Heavens" Heb 4:14 "Therefore come boldly unto the Throne of grace" Heb 4:16 "Have boldness to enter into the Holiest place by the blood of Jesus" Heb 10:19.

God said, "And ye shall seek Me, and find Me, when ye shall search for Me with all your heart" Jer 29:13. And again in the New Testament,

"Ask and it shall be given you

Seek and ye shall find

Knock and it will be

opened unto you." Mat 7:7

Jesus continues, "If you then, being evil, know how to give good gifts unto your children: how much more shall your Heavenly Father give the Holy Spirit to them that ask Him?" Luke 11:13

Yet she on earth hath union

With God, the Holy One

And mystic sweet communion

With those whose rest is won;

O happy ones and holy!

Lord, give us grace that we

Like them, the meek and lowly,

On high may dwell with Thee.

from "The Church's One Foundation"

Samuel Stone, hymn writer

--   --   --   --   --

When I was sixteen years old I visited Heaven for the first time. I was at youth camp. After the service a lot of the young people were in the back room praying together. There were a lot of people around me. We were all praying and no one was paying any attention to anyone around them. I was praying and praising the Lord for quite a while and though my eyes were closed, I could see around me. I was in a garden. There were tall slender trees with leaves growing all the way to the ground so no trunk could be seen. I was standing on green grass. There were fountains also. Directly in front of me and falling over me was a tall fountain of water. The base of this fountain was clear as crystal, delicately carved like cut glass. I could see right through it. The water from this fountain was flowing up, over and through me. It was soft, warm, invigorating and comforting.

I stepped out of the falling water and turning back around saw the head, shoulders and arms of the Lord Jesus in the water coming from this fountain. His arms were stretched out to me. Jesus stepped out of the fountain and right there we sat down on the grass to eat together, and five more people came and joined us. After a delightful picnic and time of conversation we all arose and walked to the riverbank. My back was to the river.

I seemed to know it was time for me to leave. I didn't want to leave so I asked Jesus if I could stay. Then I said, "Nevertheless, not my will, but Thine be done." I heard the Lord say, "You may come back again and again.

--   --   --   --   --

Again I was praying at home when I saw an angel near the ceiling beckon me, saying, "Come with me." The angel took me to a road that had trees on each side, like an orchard. We stepped into the grass and picked a piece of fruit the color of a peach, about two inches in diameter and perfectly round. I could hear hilarious laughter from others in the orchard. There was an opening in the trees, and beyond them was a vast plain. At the far end of the plain something very bright was approaching toward us. It stopped at the end of the trees and I saw Jesus sitting in a golden chair. The bright gold light was coming from Him.

I felt very out of place and as I looked down at myself, I saw a black form. I fell to the ground trying to hide. But Jesus said, "Arise, my child." Obediently I rose to my feet and looked. Jesus had a two-foot-long golden scepter in His right hand that He was holding out to me. As I touched the golden scepter with my right hand, I felt something go through me. Looking down I no longer saw black, but a white shining robe.

At nineteen years of age, I saw angels descending and ascending a golden stairway. They were brightly illuminated to blend with the gold of the staircase as they floated single-file down the left and up the right side. As each one came to the lowest level, he would face me and turn to go up the other side. There were no distinctions of personalities among them. Everything blended into the gold of the picture. As I stood gazing intently on each being as they occupied the lowest level one at a time, I noticed one who did have personality. She was extremely beautiful. She was dressed in a pure white garment and her hair was long, golden and full of graceful curls. She was so beautiful I could not take my eyes off of her as she began ascending the other side. I noticed how beautiful were her eyes and that she was winking at me with her right eye. Immediately I loved this sweet, innocent and pure being. She reached out and took my hand and together we ascended the golden stairs.

-- -- -- -- --

One morning, when I was twenty-three years old, after reading my Bible, during my prayer time, my companion came with a beautiful coach drawn by four beautiful white horses to take me to Heaven. Inside, the seats were comfortably cushioned with purple velvet. Too comfortable, I suppose, because I slept until we arrive at the front door of a magnificent mansion. He whispered in my ear as he helped me out of the coach We walked to the mansion and he carried me through the doorway. Inside the large lobby there were people everywhere engaged in duties of various detail. He guided me up to the next floor and we came out to a large sun porch room. One wall of this room is completely open to the beautiful countryside of Heaven. Beyond the edge of this room a porch continues with a balcony on its front edge. On each side of the porch are ivory steps going down to the park and gardens below. There are rose gardens, a swing, gazebo, pool and fountains in the yard. It is both relaxing and delightful to sit on the couch up in this room and look out over the scenery so beautiful with color and life.

Among the things we saw was a bright light outshining all the rest and moving about from place to place. As this bright light came nearer we could see it was Jesus, accompanied by a band of happy little children. Jesus came into our mansion and we found ourselves surrounded by the laughing children who made themselves right at home all over the room. We gave Jesus the seat of honor. The children were not bashful; in fact, they enjoyed being lifted up onto our laps and exchanging hugs. What one would do, another would do too. One little girl laid her head on my lap, so a little boy did the same thing. Jesus and my companion and I were talking together and enjoying His Presence and I sensed that Jesus and my companion loved each other deeply.

As I was looking around at all the infant children in the room and on the floor, Jesus stood up among them. He was dressed in white, glistening garments. Jesus was smiling and His smile seemed to pervade the room with love and happiness. The little children began to praise God by raising their hands to Jesus and singing, "Praise Jesus, praise Jesus, praise Jesus…" Even the infants on my lap reached their hands out to Jesus. My companion and I joined in with our praise and knelt before Him kissing His nail-scarred hands and feet. Jesus placed His hands on our heads and blessed us.

--   --   --   --   --

Many times in my daily prayer time I've had the privilege of visiting this beautiful mansion, giggling with my companion, watching the beautiful scenes of the City of Peace becoming more acquainted with the many rooms and entertaining Jesus in our home.

One such time we were praising God in our shining clothes, like the kind Jesus wears. Jesus appeared in the porch room where we spend the most time. He gave us a white stone. Jesus placed this stone at the heart of our being (similar to the gem-studded breastplate the priest wore.) There it will stay. It flashes excitedly whenever Jesus is near. Then He lifted us both up in His arms and dedicated us to His Father.

--   --   --   --   --

There is a rose room in this mansion that has roses growing everywhere: on the walls, in planters on the floor and hanging across the ceiling. Upstairs is my companion's desk room that has his big curved desk with room for both of us to sit behind. There is a big bay window in this room where we sit and read the Bible to each other and look out over the rainbow-colored City. And of course, there is a banquet room behind the porch room. In the porch room there is a huge organ. My companion is very musical and plays the violin, organ and sings very well. Also there is the white prayer tower that will be described later.

My companion put his arms around me as we stood in our upstairs porch room and said to me one day, "This is your home. You have no home on the earth. You will never be at home till you arrive here to stay. This will be your home for a long time. Many hundreds and thousands of years from now this will still be home. And when you come to visit me often like you do, you are coming home. You are always welcome here. This is our home."

"There are many servants in this home -- so many that each one is not busy all the time but each has only a small duty each day. So they also have plenty of time to worship God and enjoy His Heaven."

"That's beautiful" I said.

We turned around and walked back into the room from the porch area and were seated on the gold and purple cushioned furniture. A young girl quietly brought us some fruit on a tray -- dried apricots and juicy peaches. We were singing songs together about Jesus from the spontaneity of our hearts when Jesus Himself appeared with us.

"Where two or three are gathered together in My name, there I Am in the midst of them." Mat 18:20

"Jesus is always welcome in our home anytime" my companion said to me.

I arose, fell at Jesus' feet and thanked Him for His love and compassion for me and asked that I might be able to show His love to others to win them to Himself.

--　　　--　　　--　　　--　　　--

On this day, when I was twenty-four years old, we were strolling beside the crystal River on the golden street. There were many people resting on the grass beside the River and others walking on the street. We saw Jesus coming to us and ran to each side of Him. As His arm encircled me, I drew His hand up to my mouth and kissed it in gratitude, for He is our reason for being here and the Life that sustains us. We walked a while together with our arms entwined. Jesus then took some children by the hand and walked on. We watched Him for awhile. Several chariots went by with happy people in them.

My companion said, "This is the main street of Heaven. Everyone is preparing for Jesus' return to earth to gather up their loved ones who are still down there. These you see here wait to welcome loved ones now entering the gates of Heaven."

After walking another short distance, we sat on a swing where we could watch this festive gathering. Beautiful people exchanged greetings with us.

Then continuing on beside the River of Life, skipping and running along the street, my companion suggested we have a drink from the fountain of clear living water. It was delightful. Soon we came to another fountain with rainbow-colored water in it. When we drank of that we became intoxicated with laughter.

Finally we arrived at the Garden of Fountains. As we walked there, I remembered this is where I came on my first visit. Only this time I could hear the rushing water of these mighty fountains. It was very exciting to walk under the falling water, see the colors and hear the majestic music the roaring fountains make. It frightened me a little and I held tightly to my companion's arm. But it showed me how much power God can use in our behalf. We weak human beings should never doubt what our God can do. After passing several fountains we began praising the Lord with our hands raised. Soon it seemed as if the whole atmosphere were hushed before God. Looking up we saw the Lord riding overhead in a bright glistening chariot. He passed over us and we were overwhelmed with adoration and love for our Redeemer.

--   --   --   --   --

Another time we were sitting in our mansion together wearing our diamond clothes. I said, "It is every girl's dream to live happily ever after with her sweetheart in a castle and wear diamonds. Here I am enjoying all three." Then my companion and I ate some grapes and cake. After we had eaten I realized we had partaken of the communion. Then we fell silent, quietly expecting Jesus to come. "Be still

110

and know that I Am God." Psa 46:10 Soon we saw the glory of the Lord in the sky coming toward us. We welcomed Him and Jesus stood in the room before us tall, bright and glowing. He moved over to a chair and sat down. I was overwhelmed with His presence and said, "My God." Then we knelt before Him and looking up into His face I said, "My Savior. I love You, Jesus. Thank you for the suffering you endured for our salvation at Calvary." I kissed His hands that had been wounded for me.

Jesus said, "I loved you then, yes. I also love you now."

I asked Him, "What did you and Moses talk about when he went into the tent of meeting and talked to You face to face?"

Jesus said, "I Am Moses Counselor, Friend, and God."

"I love to talk to You."

Jesus said, "I give you abundantly of my Spirit."

"It is so easy to live right when I'm in your Presence."

"That's why it's so important to keep close to Me."

Then my companion and I sang a song of love to Jesus. Jesus lifted us up and placed His hands on our heads and prayed to His Father, "Father You know that I have loved them. Now let Your benediction rest on them."

--   --   --   --   --

One morning during my prayer time when I was twenty-five years old, my companion and I prayed the Lord's prayer together in the white prayer tower. This is a tall circular tower in one corner of, and structurally higher than our City Mansion, that is in the Holy Place. There are circular steps inside this tower leading up to a beautiful, soft, white room. The couches, rug, walls and furniture are all white. This is like an observatory tower with windows all around, where Heaven can be viewed, and it is a place we can go to relax alone. From here we can see the exuberant colorful fountains in the Garden of Fountains that are right outside and completely encircle the central Temple of Heaven. From the Temple were shining many colorful light rays causing a glow across Heaven and reflecting all around us in our tower. We sang a song of praise and gratitude to Jesus.

My companion was planning to go somewhere and had a twinkle in his eye. I asked to go along. So he put his arm around me and we rose into the air floating past many colorful lights until we arrived on the top step just outside the door of the Temple. There he set me down. He began guiding thousands of people safely through the doorway. These thousands of people were so enraptured with praise to God that they were not aware of much of their surroundings. The excitement in the air was so electrifying there seemed to be a strong wind. I was standing behind my companion and to keep from being blown away I held onto his waist and peeked out around him to watch. I was seeing Christians who had been tortured and killed in Communist prison camps around the world for their faith in Jesus. These saints were being ushered into the Temple of Heaven to be received before the Throne of God. How voluminous their praise! How sincere their worship to God!

Next he took me to our Chamber Mansion that is in the wall of this temple. We stood facing out of the chamber into the temple area. In our uplifted hands we were holding a bowl of sweet-smelling incense and its fragrance was rising up out of the bowl to God. We set the bowl on a high pedestal and walked back into the huge chamber. This large open front leads into a glittering room trimmed in rainbow colors. All around are crystal-clear objects One hanging on the right, he said, was a living flower. It looked like prisms of cut glass. When it moved it made beautiful music. I was happy here. We stepped into a bubbling brook running through the back of the chamber. The water was crystal clear and the bed of the brook was covered with gems sparkling with rainbow colors. We stooped down and drank some water. This caused us to praise the Lord most fervently.

He led me again to the front entrance of this chamber mansion and plopped onto a fluffy couch. He slapped the seat beside himself with his hand and grinned at me. So I sat beside him.

"Now," he said, "what were you going to ask me?"

"Well I haven't much to say after all this beauty and comfort. But why is there so much trouble on earth and here all is well with no trouble at all?"

"This is to encourage you, my dear, that there is such a real place where all is well." He put his arm around me.

"When I'm here, I'm well and healthy. When I go back I'm sick and tired. How can I serve the Lord always being tired?"

"It is not in your strength that the Lord's work is done. God's strength is made perfect in weakness. Only when self is not seen can Jesus be seen. Not in your power but only by God's power can the task be accomplished."

Jesus appeared, standing in the center of the room looking at us with deep love and tender compassion. His garments were white and glittered like they were made of millions of diamonds sewn together. Light was coming from Him, making prismatic rainbow reflections on the high diamond ceiling and walls of the chamber. The most beautiful music I ever heard was coming from within Jesus and floating gently over Heaven's atmosphere. My soul was drawn to Him.

"Hallelujah! I have found Him--

Whom my soul so long has craved!

Jesus satisfies my longings;

Through His blood I know I'm saved."

from "Satisfied"

Clara Williams, hymn writer

It seemed as if all beings in Heaven were looking to Jesus and were all praising him in deep gratitude for His great love for each of us. We knelt before Him kissing his nail-scarred hands and feet. Jesus placed His hands on our heads and blessed us.

--   --   --   --   --

Many happy times we have spent in our beautiful Chamber Mansion enjoying each other, laughing, eating together with Jesus and sharing in His love, watching the activities inside the Temple, and spending time in the Garden of Fountains just outside these Temple walls. One day we visited the school of infants also in the Temple walls. There we sat and explained to them that we were like their parents that they had left on earth. They all wanted to come and hug and kiss us. So they gathered around us and we each began lifting them to our lap, kissing and hugging each one. As we slipped away, my companion told me I had done well. But I felt so unworthy of teaching the innocents. I pray Jesus will make me pure in heart.

--   --   --   --   --

Once we were dressed in white clothes (he in a suit, I in a long dress) and went to the river on main street. My companion suggested we go into the River. So, clothes and all we waded out into the crystal clear water until it was over our heads. Under the water we could still breathe, see and hear just the same as above. The Riverbed was beautifully covered with multicolored precious stones. We were gently proceeding toward the center of Heaven. Then we turned around and faced upward. The light coming through the water made everything appear gold colored. The water and our white apparel reflected the golden hues. We floated under a golden rainbow that arched from under the water high up out of the water. Just on the other side of the archway we climbed out of the water onto the grassy bank and gave thanks to Jesus for salvation, Heaven and each other. My companion said to me, "Where did you get those colorful gems on your white dress?" Sure enough, there all over my white dress were little dazzling stones like the ones in the River.

--   --   --   --   --

One day at twenty-six years of age, my companion and I were in our white prayer tower talking.

"I wish I could learn faster. I wish I could be pleasing to you." I said.

"You please me."

"You have been living in Heaven for a while and you are so wise and I am not. You can probably see through me and see how unwise I am. Tell me some of your wisdom."

He looked down at me and said, "My wisdom is Jesus."

"Yes. Jesus is truth and love."

After a thoughtful pause I said, "Should I tell anyone about you and me?"

"Why wouldn't you?"

"They would see my faulty living and say I'm out of my mind. You are too sacred to me to have anyone make fun of or criticize."

Gently, up from the center of our room arose a clear fountain of water. It rose higher than a tall man. Then Jesus appeared in this fountain of water that melted away from around Him. "Come to Me children." He sat down and I sat beside Him. His heart was open and I could see right inside of Him to the sacred tender love. Jesus opened His heart and soul for my observation?! Isn't that too sacred for me to look on?

"Jesus, should I tell people about my companion?" My eyes watered with tears.

"Maybe they already know."

I pray I can walk worthy of the calling of God. Jesus' heart still remained open and tender toward me. "Jesus, what can I do about people I don't get along with?"

"I love those people." Jesus' heart remained open to my gaze.

"Jesus, I need sanctification in my life."

"I came to earth and lived among people. I opened My heart to them. I was tender and loving. See the marks of my visit?" He showed me His nail-scarred hands. I began to cry.

"But they can't do that to You! They can't treat You mean! Don't they know Who You are? You are God! You love them!" My tears showed how upset I was.

Then I realized my sins had been what nailed Him to the cross. How could I? But Jesus had not shut His heart to me. His heart is still open and tender. And I am to be like Him.

We laid our heads against him like John the Beloved did. We just rest in His love and drink in of His character and Spirit.

--   --   --   --   --

One time I heard the voices of the Father and Son talking. "How long, Father, till I can bring my bride home?"

And I heard the Father say, "In just a little while."

My ears were opened for a moment and I could hear all kinds of voices coming from earth. Some were desperate cries for help, some were people praising God in a church gathering, some were heart prayers and some were just noisily going about their own selfish ways. God spoke about the children of Israel in Egypt by saying, "Their cry came up before Me" (Exo 2:23) It's comforting to know God hears each of His children when they cry out to Him in prayer. How much sweeter to Him is our praise than our complaints.

--   --   --   --   --

At thirty-eight years of age I heard the most beautiful harp music. Then I saw that it was my companion, playing on the harp a Jewish song of love to El Shaddai. On the other side of the harp from me I could see Jesus sitting on the edge of the couch beaming with pleasure at the praises to Him. He was thoroughly enjoying the song of my companion.

--   --   --   --   --

Very early on a Sunday morning, I saw Jesus standing, looking through a heart-shaped rose-covered arbor doorway. His thick, curly hair was not only blonde, it was golden. His clothes were not only white, they were glowing. He is ten thousand times more handsome than the sons of men. He was looking at me but He acted as though He would walk on by in case I did not welcome Him. I saw Him and instantly smiled and beckoned Him to come into my room. He came in and sat on a chair. I sat on the floor before him and leaned against His knee looking up into His loving face. I spoke with Him openly. I held nothing back and asked Him for His advice and help. Jesus put His hand on my head and talked ever so gently. I kissed his hands that have the nail prints. "Behold, I stand at the door, and knock: if any man hear My voice, and open the door, I will come in to him, and will sup with him, and he with Me." Rev 3:20

--   --   --   --   --

One night in summer when I was very sad, I saw Jesus sitting near me. I sat at His feet, leaned my head against His knee and He laid his hand gently on my head. All through the night whenever I woke up He was still there with His hand on my head. "Lo (My name in short form), I Am with you always, even unto the end of the world." Mat 28:20 "Amen. Even so, come, Lord Jesus." Rev 22:20

--   --   --   --   --

"When Thou saidst, seek ye My face; my heart said unto Thee, Thy face, Lord, will I seek." Psa 27:8

Safe in the arms of Jesus,

Safe on His gentle breast,

There by His love o'ershaded,

Sweetly my soul shall rest.

Fanny J. Crosby, hymn writer

THE PLANTING OF THE LORD

by Joy Hetrick (Oden's Daughter)

"Here we have not a permanent city, but we <u>SEEK</u> one to come."
Heb 13:14 Abraham considered earth a foreign country, because He
knew of a City built by God. (Heb 11:8-10) The story of Abraham is
one of my favorite Bible stories.

DID ABRAM BELIEVE? REALLY??

While Abram was still in idol worshipping country, Yahweh called
him out, and told him to leave his country and his relatives. Yahweh
said, "You start traveling and I will show you where your destination
is to be." How's that for adventure?! Anyone want to sign up with
that travel agent?!? Evidently Abram believed Yahweh was totally trustworthy because he obeyed and went out not knowing where he was
going. (Heb 11:8)

He probably prayed more than once 'Show me Your path, Yahweh." When he came to the land of Canaan, Yahweh gave him a promise -- "<u>THIS</u> is the land I will give to your descendants, walk around
in it, up and down, and all the way across." (Gen 13:16-17) So Abram
traveled all around considering it a foreign country, and received no
inheritance in it. (Acts 7:5)

Why did he consider it a foreign country? Didn't he believe what
Yahweh told him? If believing is to be so convinced that you live differ-
ently, then yes, Abram certainly believed. In fact he believed so firmly,
that he was considered righteous. And evidently Yahweh was pleased

with the obedience of his faith, because his testimony of Abram was, "he is My friend". (Jam 2:23 & II Chron 20:7) So Abram, along with Isaac and Jacob considered it a foreign country because they were ALL wise enough to see beyond this earthly life, and SEEK a better country, NOT the one they came from. They all lived in temporary dwellings, (tents) declaring plainly they were strangers here and LOOKING FOR a city with foundations, whose builder and maker is God. (*By the way ---- tents have no permanent foundation do they?!?!*) They were convinced that Yahweh had prepared a better country for them.

And since they believed, and DESIRED a heavenly country, the Bible says, **Yahweh is not ashamed to be called their God**; for He has prepared for them a City. (Heb 11:13-16) By the obedience of their faith they pleased Yahweh.

Then many years later when Yahshua/Jesus humbled Himself, became a man and lived among us, what did He say? "I Am the God of Abraham, and the God of Isaac, and the God of Jacob."! (Mat 33:32) Sounds like He was pleased to be called their God!! Still to this day, after another 2000 years, how do we know Yahweh/God?? As the God of Abraham, Isaac, and Jacob. Now what about you and me? Are we going to believe so firmly that Yahweh is totally trustworthy, and prove it by our obedience? What will Yahweh's testimony be of me? Would He want to be called my God?

<u>If Yahweh, who knows MY heart, was on the witness stand, what would His testimony be of ME?</u>

The eyes of Yahweh look back and forth through the whole earth. to show Himself strong in behalf of them whose heart is **completely His.** (II Chronicles 16:9)

Wouldn't it be exciting to go on a journey of faith with an all-powerful, all-wise, Friend who created you and loves you? Someone you could totally trust, and joyfully obey? Oh what a witness you could be to everyone around you, of His salvation, his love, His instructions for this life, and the promise of eternal life in Heaven!! Well I say -- let's all sign up with that travel agent!!

Make ME to go I the path of Thy COMMANDMENTS; for therein do I DELIGH<u>T</u>. Psa 119:35

"One thing I HAVE DESIRED of the Lord, that will I SEEK after: that I MAY DWELL in the house of the LORD all the days of my life, to behold the beauty of the LORD, and to inquire in his Temple." Psa 27:4

"We have in Heaven a better and an enduring substance." (Heb.10:34). Heaven is a place of everlasting, exquisite beauty. There are many mansions, flowers, Tree of Life, fountains, the River, etc. But let me tell you of my favorite garden, where I love to go.

*** *** *** *** *** *** ***

There are artistically arranged colorful flowers bordering a soft golden pathway, in a large beautiful garden. At one end of the garden is a clear, rippling brook, though not made of water, that is exhilarating when one is immersed. In the center of this garden is a large circle of soft, dark and light green bushes, with a parting on one side for an entrance. These bushes are high enough to come together at the top, forming a roof. Inside are white seats to accommodate many delightful visits with Jesus.

This garden is attached to one side of an "apartment-like" structure or Chamber Mansion. Its walls are like translucent glass with colors intricately woven throughout. In one room is a fancy white table with rounded edges where we have "tea parties". All its furnishings are comfortably designed to make you feel contentedly at home.

On the other end of this Chamber Mansion is a full-length "doorway" that opens into the Most Holy Place. It was out this "doorway" I was gazing one day when my attention was captured by a fascinating scene, on the sea of glass, in front of the Throne. At first all I saw looked like the raised hands of many people waving. Looking closer, I saw that it was many people forming the shape of a tree. The top part, that would be likened to its leaves, was slowly and gracefully waving back and forth before the Lord. It made my own heart overflow with wonder, and praise, and I joined in the worship to my Blessed Redeemer.

Isaiah 61:3 "...to give to them beauty for ashes, the oil of joy for mourning, the garment of praise for the spirit of heaviness; **that they might be called trees of righteousness, the planting of the Lord, that he might be glorified.**

*** *** *** *** *** *** ***

One day my companion and I we were looking out the picture "doorway" of our chamber mansion and saw saints, wearing golden garments singing beautiful music while forming a glistening, golden candlestick formation, like the one in the tabernacle. I watched this fascinating scene, til the candlestick was all in place, **except**, for the flame.

So the thought came to me, where is the fire for the candlestick. Then as the flame appeared I understood with great awe and wonder, that it was the Holy Spirit as tongues of fire, making it complete and showing His delight and acceptance of the saints' worship. (Acts 2:2, 3)

*** *** *** *** *** *** ***

One of the first things Dad taught us was to adopt children in Heaven. There are many reasons why babies go to Heaven, and sadly enough, some of them will never see their earthly parents. So over the years I have been able to adopt many children. At the end of the class, one by one, each child gets special attention and a hug. There have been times after the hugs that the children, have poured flowers like soft sparkly jewels, all over us. One time they put on me an elaborate crown made of flowers and jewels, with something like a veil on the back. And I heard a voice say, "The bride and bridegroom are about to be joined."

Sometimes these children will sing at the banquets in our mansion. Other times they come visit us in our City Mansion. They are delightfully obedient and precious children.

121

One day I arrived in a field of brilliantly colored flowers that looked like sparkling jewels. I was by myself and sat down to gaze at this artistic loveliness, breathe the pure air, and enjoy the blissful peace. Off in the distance I saw what looked like a bright cloud approaching. Very soon I was overwhelmed by a large group of my children surrounding me, and 'smothering' me with hugs and kisses, laughing and giggling the whole time. By now I was laying down on the soft 'ground'. When I was able to see thru the cloud of children, I saw my companion standing there chuckling, with a grin from ear to ear.

I reached up my hand to him, saying playfully, "Rescue me, rescue me!!"

He reached down his hand pulled me up to sit and sat down beside me. The children were all eager for my attention, but patiently and in an orderly fashion they were taking turns. Some showed me pictures they drew, some had harps they made and played, others did somersaults. Then they thrilled us with melodious songs of perfect harmony. It was a heavenly luxury to spend time with those pure, sweet charming children. To be sure, children are one of the many delights of Heaven.

✳✳✳ ✳✳✳ ✳✳✳ ✳✳✳ ✳✳✳ ✳✳✳ ✳✳✳

During a time in my life of very intense spiritual battles, while in my prayer time, I was shown the golden stairway to Heaven with angels going up and down, in my behalf. And I had right beside me a special colorful angel -- I do not know if this was one of my guardian angels becoming visible or another one. I would encourage you to remember that there is always interaction between Heaven and earth on our behalf. (Psa 91:11 & Psa 34:7) Angels are ministering spirits to heirs of salvation. There are many instances in the Bible of angels interacting with people of earth -- Abraham, Gideon, Peter and many more. So even though you may not see your angels, they are with you just the same! It's another proof of our Father's love and care for us.

✳✳✳ ✳✳✳ ✳✳✳ ✳✳✳ ✳✳✳ ✳✳✳ ✳✳✳

Now I invite you to join me for a picnic!!

It must have been because of the intense battles I was having, that Yahshua came and carried me to Heaven. I was sitting on Yahshua's lap, my head on His shoulder, with my companion sitting beside Him, and thinking I was in our Chamber Mansion. I was wanting to have a nice quiet talk, to pour out my troubles, and ask for his help when I sensed something was going on. Opening my eyes and looking at my companion, I saw him standing up and reaching out his hand to me. When I got up, took his hand and looked around there were people everywhere! With my earth troubles still clinging to my spirit, I confess I was a little disappointed about not having a private talk. But Yahweh knew exactly what I needed.

So I turned to my companion and said, "Why are all these people here?"

He replied with a winning smile, "We are outside of our city mansion, and a picnic is being prepared" *(Now I LOVE picnics)* So I brightened up, became the gracious hostess, and began welcoming everyone.

People began to head toward the back yard area where there were tables covered with soft white cloths, and decorated with blue and purple borders. On the tables were flower bouquets of all colors and blue and purple platters filled with food. I remember a kind of fruit pudding, apples, and a nut butter on a type of biscuit. There was grape nectar and something like white milk to drink. There was more food but that's all I took notice to.

When everyone had gathered in the back yard, Yahshua appeared, blessed the food, and the fellowship continued as we ate. Yahshua began to move about among the people sharing joy and laughter. He was the most honored and most loved guest. There were also many other guests, including my Dad, and my Mom, and another lady that I worked with many years back, who has encouraged me to share these things with you

So what did I do? Well what do you think you would do? I sat close by my companion on a most comfortable little chair, and ate a little. But mostly I just sat there with adoring eyes and contented smile watching Yahshua, with not an ounce of thought about earthly cares. Every now and then He turned and smiled at me, communicating with His thoughts, *"I know all about your life, I AM with you, just trust me."*

After a little while, some of our adopted children delighted us with some beautiful worship songs with motions. After the concert as the guests left, I interacted with them and thanked them for coming. Then I had to return to earth.

Now I will explain why I didn't have a private talk about my troubles. Because I was focusing on my problems instead of on my gracious Father, who already had the problem solved.

*** *** *** *** *** *** ***

During one of my visits with Jesus, we were out in the Holy Place, sitting on the grass among the trees talking and laughing. There were other friends with us who were also extremely happy. Everyone was enjoying the delights of Heaven.

With a longing in my heart to be forever with them, I looked up at Jesus and asked, "How long will it be until you gather your saints and bring them home?"

Looking at me with a radiant smile, He replied with a chuckle, "Very soon now."

Then as if not able to contain Himself any longer, He began to laugh. This caused everyone around to join in hilarious laughter! The atmosphere of Heaven is so peaceful and always joyful. Oh, what a day that will be when Jesus takes me by the hand and leads me to my Heavenly Home, to stay forever. What a glorious day that will be!

MY GUARDIAN ANGELS

by Gladys Hetrick (Oden's Daughter)

Some years ago, while working at a temporary job in downtown St. Petersburg, Florida, I had to ride the city bus. This is not the safest of situations, but my mother's prayers followed me daily.

One day during that time, the Lord opened my spiritual eyes in a very exciting way! I could see that two very tall angels, one on each side of me accompanied me, and just a little ahead of me. They were seven feet tall, had golden hair and wore long garments that were the brightest white -- whiter than snow. I could only see a glimpse of their faces, but they seemed to be very handsome.

Later, when I realized I had actually seen angels, I was overwhelmed and thanked the Lord for the reassurance of His protection.

"He shall give His angels charge over thee ... to keep thee in all thy ways." Psalm 91:11

STEPPING IN THE RIVER

by Faith Hetrick (Oden's Daughter)

Having heard soul-stirring stories about Heaven from my earliest childhood, and being encouraged by my Dad, Oden Hetrick, to "set your affection on things above where Christ sitteth on the right hand of God" Colossians 3:2 and to "look not at the things which are seen, but at the things which are not seen (eternal realities) " 2 Corinthians 4:18, I have endeavored to do just that. The Lord has given me many brief glimpses into that Heavenly City.

One such experience came after a time of fasting and prayer. I found myself on the grassy bank of a beautiful quiet stream. I knew this must be part of the River of Life and the thing to do was to walk down into it, which I did, until even my head was under the "water." The sensation was indescribable, but it felt like my very soul and spirit were being cleansed and refreshed. Coming up out of the water onto the opposite bank, I was filled with pure joy and laughter like I never knew before!

Not only does the Lord have ways of preparing us for Heaven in this life, but even after we get there, He has provided all we need to prepare us more fully to enter into the joys of that eternal Kingdom. He really does "think of everything!"

PART THREE

END TIME EVENTS

**By comparing 77 passages of Scripture that describe
The Day of the Lord,
the following order of events is what we found.**

Christians in many lands are suffering tribulation, so what does the Church escape? Christians of all ages have suffered tribulation -- some more, some less. But many American Christians know very little about tribulation even though Jesus said, "In the world you will have tribulation." John 16:33. It is from the GREAT tribulation that we are promised escape and deliverance -- a 3 & 1/2-year time of wrath at the end of this age. Rev 13:5 says it is "42 months." Dan 12:7 says it is "time, times and half a time." Daniel's 70 weeks <u>include</u> the atonement for iniquity (Dan 9:24). And Jesus did not fulfill this until <u>after</u> the 69th week. (Dan 9:26)

When Jesus spoke to four of His disciples about the end of the age He described four events that will happen in quick succession just before the GREAT tribulation.

1: CAPTURE OF JERUSALEM

2: WORLDWIDE DARKNESS

3: HIS APPEARING

4: RAPTURE OF ELECT

After Jesus described "these things" He said,

"When you <u>see</u> <u>these</u> <u>things</u>, realize that it (redemption/rapture) is near, even at the doors." Mat

24:33

"When these things begin to come to pass...your redemption (resurrection/rapture) is near." Lke 21:28

"When you see these things come to pass, realize that the kingdom (City) of God is near at hand (soon to appear)." Lke 21:31

Evidently rapture saints will see "these things" come to pass. So if you are still here when the world gets dark, don't be afraid; just stay inside and watch and pray. The darkness will only last about three days; and according to Jesus, your redemption (rapture) will then be very near.

"These things" are outlined below. They follow the beginning of sorrows described in Mt 24:7-8, Mrk 13:8 & Lke 21:9.

PROGRAM OF END TIME EVENTS   TIME FRAME

1: ARMIES INVADE ISRAEL   *---FEW DAYS*

AND CAPTURE JERUSALEM

(see Ezk 38 Jol 2 Zec 14:2-7 Mrk 13:14)

Ezk 38:18-20   "It will be at the same time when Gog comes against the land of Israel, says the Lord God, that my fury will be aroused...on that day the land of Israel will be greatly shaken...and everyone on the face of the earth will shake at My presence (appearing).

Lke 21:20   "When you see Jerusalem surrounded by armies, then realize that its desolation is near." (This is the abomination of desolation spoken of by Daniel the prophet in Dan 9:27. Compare Mat 24:15)

129

2: LITERAL DARKNESS ---ABOUT THREE DAYS WILL COVER THE EARTH

(see Jol 2:1-3, 9-10, 20, 31 Act 2:20 Rev 6:12-13)

*Isa 60:2 *"Darkness will cover the earth and gross darkness the people"*

*Jol 3:14-16 *"The day of the Lord is near...the sun and the moon will be darkened, and the stars will not shine."*

*Jn 9:4 *Jesus said, "The night is coming when no man can work."*

2a: THIS DARKNESS WILL IMMEDIATELY FOLLOW THE INVASION TRIBULATION

(See Psa 18:3-28 2Sa 22:1-27)

*Jol 2:5-10 *"...a strong people in battle array...they shall run here and there in the City (Jerusalem)...the earth will quake before them: the sky will tremble: the sun and the moon and the stars will be darkened."*

*Mat 24:29 *"Immediately following the tribulation of those days the sun will be darkened, the moon will not shine, and stars (meteorites) will fall from the sky, and the powers of the sky will be shaken."* (This verse refers to the capture of Jerusalem and the darkness "immediately following." Do not change "tribulation of those <u>days</u>" to GREAT tribulation of 3, 1/2 <u>years</u>.)

2b: THE EARTH AND PLANETS   ---FEW DAYS

WILL BE MOVED OUT OF ORBIT AT THIS TIME

*Job 9:6 *"He shakes the earth out of its place"*

*Isa 13:13 *"I will shake the sky (planet area) and the earth will be moved out of its place, in the wrath of the Lord of hosts, in the day of His fierce anger."*

3: GOD AND JESUS WILL APPEAR IN THE SKY

IN THE CITY OF GOD --FOLLOWING DARKNESS

(This is the 48-hour "day of the Lord") (See Psa 48:1-8 Psa 97:1-6 Isa 40:5 Act 2:20 Rev 12:10-12, 20:11, 21:2, 22:3)

*Mat 24:29-30 *"The sun will be darkened, the moon will give no light, and stars (meteorites) will fall from the sky, and the powers of the sky (planet area) will be shaken. Then the sign of the Son of Man will appear in the sky."* (The "sign" is the City and Throne of God.)

*Mat 26:64 *"Hereafter you will <u>see</u> the Son of Man sitting at the right hand of Power (God on His Throne) and coming on (appearing among) the clouds of the sky."* (See Psa 110:1)

3a: RAPTURE IMMEDIATELY   ---HOUR OR SO

FOLLOWS APPEARING

(See Mat 6:13 Mrk 13:26-27 Lke 21:36 Jhn 14:3 I Th 4:13-17 2Tm 4:18 Rev 3:10)

*Mat 24:30-31 *"Then shall appear in the (sky) the sign (City) of the Son of Man (Jesus)...And He will send His angels with a great trumpet sound, who will gather together His elect from the four winds, from one end of the (sky) to the other."*

HEAVEN

131

*1Jn 3:2 *"We know that when He appears we will be like Him."* (See Jhn 14:3 Col 3:4 1Pt 5:4 1Jn 2:28)

*Rev 12:10 *"Now has come...the Kingdom (City) of our God, and the power of His Christ....Therefore rejoice you skies and you (including raptured saints) who dwell in them. But woe to those who inhabit the earth and the sea! For the devil has come down to you, having great wrath because he knows that his time is short."* (3&1/2 years)

4: GREAT TRIBULATION --FOLLOWS APPEARING & RAPTURE

(This is the 3&1/2-year "day of the Lord" or "time of wrath" -- the things that raptured saints escape. See Lke 21:36)

*Jol 2:31 *"The sun will be turned into darkness and the moon into blood <u>before</u> the great and terrible day of the Lord comes."*

*Rev 6:12-17 *"The sun became black as sackcloth of hair, the moon became as blood, and stars (meteorites) fell to earth... and the sky (planet area) was rolled back like a scroll...and everyone (left on earth)... hid themselves in caves and rocks and mountains. And they cried to the mountains and to the rocks, Fall on us and hide us from the face of Him who sits on the Throne, and from the wrath of the Lamb. Because the <u>great</u> day of their wrath has now come, and who will be able to stand?"*

*Rev 13:5-7 *"And he (sea beast) was allowed to exercise authority for forty-two months (3&1/2 years). And with his mouth he blasphemed God, and His Name, and His dwelling place and those (including raptured saints) who <u>dwell in the sky</u>. And he was allowed to make war with the saints (on the earth) and to overcome them."* Verse 18, *"And his number is 666."*

So *"these things"* in the question of the disciples, and in the *answer of Jesus -- "these things" that pinpoint the very end of the age, begin with armies invading Israel (Ezk 38).*

"When these things begin to come to pass, lift up your heads and look up, because your redemption is very near." Lke 21:28

(Our <u>souls</u> must be redeemed now -- washed from sins in Jesus blood -- our <u>bodies</u> are redeemed when Jesus appears.)

"Behold, I come quickly, and My reward is with Me to give every person according to their work. Blessed are those who wash their robes and keep His commandments, that they may have right to the tree of Life and may enter through the gates into the City." Rev 22:12 & 14

"Let us therefore fear, lest a promise being left to us of entering into His rest, any of you should seem to come short of it." Heb 4:1

WHO IS JESUS?

Song of Solomon 5:16 *He is altogether lovely.*

Isaiah 9:6 *His name shall be called Wonderful, Counselor, the Might God, the Everlasting Father, the Prince of Peace.*

Isaiah 53:5 *He was wounded for our transgression, He was bruised for our iniquities: the chastisement of our peace was upon him; and with His stripes we are healed.*

Matthew 3:17 *A voice from Heaven said, This is My Beloved Son, in whom I Am delighted*

Matthew 16:16 *You are the Christ the Son of the Living God.* PETER

John 1:1-4 *The Word (Jesus) was with God in the beginning, and the Word was God. Everything was made by Him and nothing was made without Him. He brought Life and Light to men, and darkness cannot stop this Light from shining.*

John 1:14 *The Word became flesh and lived a little while with us, and we saw the glory of God's only Son, full of love and truth.*

John 6:69 *We believe and know that You are the Holy One of God.*

Colossians 1:15-17 *He is exactly like God who is unseen. He is before and above all creation. He made everything, both seen and unseen, in Heaven and on earth -- thrones,* *dominions, rulers and powers -- everything was made by Him and for Him and He holds it together.*

Colossians 1:19 *It was God's will that divine fullness should dwell in him.*

Hebrews 1:6 *Let all the angels of God worship Him.*

Hebrews 1:8 *To the Son He says, Your throne O God is forever and ever.*

I John 5:1 *Everyone who believes that Jesus is the Christ, is God's child.*

Revelation 19:16 *He is King of kings and Lord of lords.*

ABOUT THE HOLY CITY BUILT BY GOD

Psalm 48:2 *It is Mt. Zion on the sides of the North, the City of the Great King.*

Matthew 4:17 & Mark 1:14-15 *It is the heaven where our Father in Heaven abides*

Matthew 13:43 *It is the kingdom of our Father, where the righteous will shine like the sun.*

Matthew 16:28 *Jesus will return in this kingdom.*

Matthew 24:29-30 *It is the sign of Jesus that appears in the sky after the darkness.*

Matthew 24:35 *This heaven does NOT pass away.*

Matthew 25:10 *Here the Bridegroom is married.*

Matthew 25:31 *It is the Throne of Jesus' Glory.*

Matthew 25:34 *It is the kingdom made before the world and inherited by the spiritual saints.*

Matthew 26:29 *It is the Father's kingdom where Jesus will drink new wine with His disciples*

John 14:2 *It is our Father's house of mansions,*

Jesus calls it, "My Father's House"

I Corinthians 15:50 *It is the kingdom where flesh and blood cannot enter.*

Galatians 4:26 *It is the Jerusalem that is above*

Ephesians 5:5 *It is the kingdom of Christ and God*

Hebrews 11:10 *It's the City with foundations, looked for by Abraham, designed and built by God*

Hebrews 12:28 *It is the kingdom that can't be shaken*

Revelation 4:2-3 *It is God's Throne in the sky*

Revelation 11:19 *It is God's Temple in the sky*

Revelation 13:6 *It is God's Tabernacle in the sky*

Revelation 20:11 *It is the Great White Throne in the sky (2nd heaven) where God sits when earth and its sky (1st heaven) flee from His face.*

Revelation 21:1 *The new heaven is earth's remade sky.*

Revelation 21:2 *It is the new Jerusalem*

Revelation 21:9 *It is the Bride, the Lamb's wife.*

THE CITY WAS MADE BEFORE THE WORLD

Enoch 68:24 *Heaven was suspended by an oath for ever, before the world was made.*

Matthew 25:34 *Jesus said to His sheep, Inherit the kingdom, made for you from earth's foundations.*

Hebrews 4:3 *The work to build it (this City of rest) was finished from the foundation of the world.*

THE CITY BUILT BY GOD WILL BE ESTABLISHED BY HIM FOREVER IN THE SKY LIKE THE SUN AND THE MOON

Psalm 48:2 *Mt. Zion on the sides of the north.*

Psalm 48:8 *God will establish the City forever.*

Psalm 78:69 *He built His sanctuary like high palaces, like the earth, to last forever.*

Psalm 89:36-37 *David's throne will be established forever in the sky like the sun and like the moon.*

Isaiah 33:15-16 *The righteous shall dwell on high.*

Isaiah 33:17 *You will see the King in His beauty, and behold the land that is very far off.*

Amos 9:6 *The Lord builds His chambers in the sky.*

Matthew 8:11 *The kingdom of heaven (the sky).*

II Corinthians 5:1 *A building of God, eternal in the skies.*

Revelation 4:2 *A throne was set in the sky.*

Revelation 11:19; Rev 14:17; Rev 15:5; Rev 16:17 *The temple of God in the sky (seen by men on earth)*

Revelation 20:11 *Earth and sky flee from the face of God on His Throne in the sky.*

THE CITY IS BIG, BRIGHT AND BEAUTIFUL

Psalm 48:2 *Beautiful -- the joy of the whole earth.*

Revelation 4:2-3 *A Throne was set in the sky with a Bright Being upon it, and a rainbow around it.*

Revelation 21:10--22:5 *It is a City of Gold, foursquare, a cube 12,000 furlongs (1500 miles) on each side. Its 12 gates are each 1 pearl with 1 angel and the name of 1 Israeli tribe; 12 different jewels cover the 12 foundations like a rainbow and contain the 12 apostles' names. Its tree of life is on both banks of the crystal River and has one fruit for each of the 12 months. The streets of gold are just beyond the trees on each side of the river. The City has no night for the Throne and Light and Glory of God and Jesus are there where the saints live and reign forever.*

WHO LIVES IN THE HOLY CITY?

Matthew 7:21 *Those who do the will of God in Heaven.*

John 3:5 *Except a man be born of water and of the Spirit, he cannot enter into the kingdom of God.*

Hebrews 4:3 *We who have believed do enter into rest.*

Revelation 21:27 *Those written in the Lamb's Book of Life*

Revelation 21:24 *Those who are saved.*

Revelation 21:9 *The Bride, the Lamb's wife.*

WITH WHAT BODY DO THEY COME? (I Cor 15:35)

Romans 8:17 *glorified*
I Corinthians 15:42 *incorruptible*
    43 *glorious and powerful*
    44 *spiritual*
    49 *Heavenly image*
    53 *immortal*
Philippians 3:21 *glorious*

HOW LONG WILL THEY BE THERE?

Psalm 23:6 *I will dwell in God's house forever*

Psalm 61:4 *I will abide in Thy Tabernacle forever*

II Corinthians 5:1 *When this earthly body fails, we have a better body made by God, eternal in the skies.*

Revelation 3:12 *Overcomers will be made pillars in the temple of God, and go no more out.*

Revelation 22:1-5 *Saints reign forever in Holy City.*

SOME ACTIVITIES IN THE CITY

Psalm 16:11 *In Thy Presence is fullness of joy; at Thy right hand are pleasures forevermore.*

Psalm 36:8 *Saints will be filled and satisfied with the abundance of God's house. They shall drink from His River of pleasures.*

Psa 37:4, 5 *Delight yourself in Him and He will give you the desires of your heart.*

Matthew 8:11 *Saints will sit down with Abraham and Isaac and Jacob in the kingdom of the sky.*

Matthew 25:21 *You have been faithful over a few things. I will make you ruler over many things. Enter into the joy of your Lord.*

Matthew 26:29 *I'll not drink of this vine fruit till I drink it new with you in My Father's kingdom.*

Luke 6:21 *Those who weep now shall laugh.*

Jude 24 *He is able to present you faultless before His* *glorious Presence with exceeding joy.*

Revelation 2:7 & 22:2 *Eat fruit from the Tree of Life*

Revelation 2:17 *Overcomers will eat hidden manna.*

Revelation 3:5 *Overcomers will be dressed in white and presented by name to the Father and his angels.*

Revelation 3:4 & 21 *Overcomers will walk with Jesus in white clothing and sit with Him in His throne.*

Revelation 7:17 *The Lamb shall feed them.*